010504

The McKenzie Scott Executive Job Search System

2004 Edition

Our Client Handbook — Part I

by Bob Gerberg

About This Book

Designed to be easy to read, this book covers the principles of the McKenzie Scott system. Thanks to the worldwide reach of the Internet, 250,000 people will read extensive portions of this book online. In addition, including complimentary copies, more than 250,000 copies will be shipped worldwide, making this the most widely read publication on the executive job search process.

 Publication date January 5, 2004. Library of Congress Catalog Card Number 2003111837, ISBN 0-9745114-1-2 (soft cover). ISBN 0-9745114-0-4 (hard cover). Published by McKenzie Scott Press, 7979 East Tufts Avenue Parkway, Ste. 1400, Denver, CO 80237 • 800-320-1277 • Fax 303-770-8639

Table of Contents

Millions of Job Seekers Have These Potentially Dangerous Misconceptions

"I think my resume is really good."
"My friends say I'll do great."
"I can always get a job with my network."
"Sending out a lot of resumes is all I need."
"All I'll need to do is start answering ads."
"Recruiters will be after someone like me."
"If I get the interview, I'll get the job."
"I'm very good at negotiating."
"I'll only be out of work 6-8 weeks."

Millions of Job Seekers Make These Equally Dangerous Assumptions

"My field is slow. I don't know how to change industries."
"I just don't have the right contacts."
"There's nothing available in the market."
"My industry is contracting... there's nothing there."
"My age is the whole problem."
"I'm too specialized."
"Everyone says I'm overqualified."
"The image of being unemployed is holding me back."
"I need to wait until the economy comes back."
"I don't have the educational credentials they want."

The Plight of Today's Professional and Executive Job Seeker

Each year for the past 15 years, in good economies and bad, the time it takes the average job seeker to find a new position has grown longer.

About ten years ago, *Time* magazine featured a cover story titled *Finding the Great American Job... The Rules of the Game Have Changed Forever.* Since that time, every major American business publication has weighed in, offering their thoughts along a similar vein.

From time to time, the U.S. Labor Department and other government agencies have put out doom and gloom statistics... all relating to how long it takes people to find jobs in America. In June of 2003, with 132 million employed, the government said that 9 million Americans were out of work, while the *New York Times* claimed that 6 million more were not included in these statistics... because they had given up.

A newsletter in the staffing industry proclaims that 30 million people circulate resumes each month, while the number of jobs coming on the market (at professional and executive levels) is less than 10% of that number.

With this in mind, let's examine the plight of many of today's executive and professional job seekers on a closer basis. What's the problem?

When people look for a job, many are under time and financial pressure to find something quickly. They start thinking about finding a new job with some apprehension... but also a guarded optimism—because they think they know how to do it. *Unfortunately, most do not!*

To begin with, many don't really know which industries and industry segments would be their best targets. Industries and jobs are continually changing and nothing seems as permanent as it used to be. We've all observed that today's high-flying company can be bankrupt, bought out, or passed by in just a few years. Famous name corporations seem to come and go faster than ever before.

Even more basic, many job seekers don't know how they compare to their competition. They're not really aware of their most saleable strengths, and while they've heard about transferable skills... they probably have never analytically approached what they can bring to the market—outside of their industry. In short, they really don't know how and where they match up... or quite what to do about it.

Not only that, they are never really sure if their resume presents them in the best light... if it's formatted correctly for electronic transmission... if they have the right keywords for scanning and search software—or if they need more than one resume.

Making things worse is the fact that some people end up spending a lot of time answering ads on the Internet, a long-shot proposition at best… as up to 200 others respond to each attractive position. This involves too many hours of work, especially when people don't have great materials… and they get little or nothing to show for it.

Unfortunately, the Internet is a two-edged sword. The vast news available is undeniable… and the potential sources of information are unbelievably numerous.

But, as almost everyone finds out, you can spend endless hours *and not really get to the information that you need* for a job search.

As they begin to think more about how to find the right new job, they also slowly realize that they aren't sure how to identify the growth companies, start-ups, medium and large employers… that are truly their best prospects… or the decision makers to contact.

The tragedy is, they will never access more than an incredibly small fraction of the total jobs that are available right now… and which might be suitable for them.

Now, of course, there are traditional ways to connect with jobs… including unpublished jobs. But they involve endless networking… the method of choice recommended by most outplacement counselors… but which to some is a demeaning and extremely time consuming process.

Most people are totally unaware of the new ways to connect with suitable jobs... because they don't have access to the right technology or resources—and they've never done it before.

In addition, as they probably know... deep down... without really being connected, they simply don't know how to penetrate what they've heard is the "unpublished market"... where 50% of all openings will be filled... and with much less competition.

Adding to all of this, there's another problem when it comes to interviewing. Even though they may have good personal skills, they're probably not experienced in competitive interviewing and negotiating. Here we mean situations where 10 other well-qualified people are in the running for each good job. They simply don't have enough hours in the day!

The Onset of the "AFD" Syndrome

It's small wonder that many who look for new jobs have developed what we refer to as AFD… or Anxiety… which turns to Fear… which turns to Dread.

Every day, people read about thousands of their peers losing jobs, searching for many months, then finally giving up. They read about or see marriages crumble, children taken out of schools, homes sold, and people moving from an area to avoid humiliation.

When they talk to others *who have not been able to find a job—much less a suitable job,* they see in their faces and hear something in their voices that is disconcerting to say the least. It's what can only be described as a feeling of guilt and hopelessness.

Some read general news about a *"jobless recovery,"* where portions of the economy thrive but do not produce a demand for talents that were sought after a few short years ago. Others read about companies *"using technology"* to improve productivity and eliminate jobs at all levels. They also read about high-level jobs being exported to other countries and about *"outsourcing."*

As more companies develop global computer networks, as parts of business become more data intensive, as telecommunications on an international basis continue to improve and get much cheaper, it won't be just software engineering jobs that are exported to Asia and elsewhere. All types of office and administrative jobs, accounting, market analysis, tax work and jobs requiring CPAs and so on will soon be exported. In gut terms, this simply means many large employers will be finding ways to use technology to hire for less or reduce the need for the millions of jobs they needed a few years ago.

For someone who knows he or she is going to need a new job, it's small wonder that all of this produces stress, which is simply based on ***"anxiety."***

Even if they have jobs, quite a few are anxious that they might not have them for long. And, it's precisely when they are let go, or come to believe that their job is at risk... that what was previously ***"just anxiety"*** ...begins to turn to ***"fear."*** The reason is also simple. They know they are going to begin to search for a job in a market that has left so many talented others stranded and broken.

Indeed, once they start searching, if they are not successful after a few months, then that's when ***"fear"***... actually begins to turn to ***"dread."***

Dread is when they begin to realize they've done all they know how to do... with all that they know that worked in the past... and have still not succeeded. It's when they begin to comprehend that their standard of living might be drastically and permanently lowered. It's not an easy thing to contemplate.

Let's First Look at Some Services Which Have "Not Proven" to Be the Solution to This Problem

There are thousands of people and services that have tried to offer solutions to this problem. First are the ***career counseling firms***, who also go by such names as career marketing or executive marketing firms and career management firms.

Now, there are good career counselors, but whether you retain a local or national counseling firm, all the real help you will get is strictly limited to the "how to" advice of a single counselor—*for better or worse!*

Since these firms don't possess a wealth of other resources, their staff emphasizes networking as the predominant strategy for getting a job. *Networking, networking and more networking*... as some people describe it. They say it's the way to attack the "hidden" job market. This rather interesting but deceptive term, widely used by representatives of some career counseling firms, has a somewhat clandestine or shadowy feel to it. Of course, there is nothing hidden about it, as we'll discuss!

A much smaller category of assistance includes the ***resume mailing firms***. They write a historical resume, attach it to a five-line cover letter and mass mail it to firms by SIC code. However, large numbers of users report these "shot-gun" services produce disastrous results.

A third category of firms includes ***job listing subscriptions***... where publishers obtain listings from recruiters and reprint them. Now, recruiters account for 9% of all openings. These subscription services provide access to a small slice of this market—openings people might not otherwise access. However, the concept is flawed. Obviously, the more successful the subscription services are, the greater the competition experienced by each of their subscribers.

A fourth major category of assistance involves the ***traditional outplacement services.*** As a concept, these firms began to catch on in the late 1970s and early 1980s, but very little has changed since then. When organizations let people go, they pay outplacement firms to make available job hunting counselors and a place to go.

Typically, people get to use shared cubicles or offices and attend workshops and get counseling advice. Most outplacement staff are temporary contractors.

Outplacement has its roots in a legal and public relations concept. Firms wish to avoid legal costs associated with terminations and they want to keep some goodwill in their communities. But in a unique twist for any service industry... no guarantees of satisfactory service are provided to individuals—*the ones receiving the service!*

Today, it is a $2 billion industry. Critics of outplacement also point out that these services are antiquated and really don't do much for the individual. And, *they don't relieve them of any of the real hard work of job hunting*.

For example, traditional outplacement services are not going to professionally write your resumes… connect you to the openings, leads and contacts you need… or market your resumes broadly to employers, growth firms, VCs and so on. These firms have failed to embrace the technology breakthroughs that have swept through the employment field and most others.

But, this criticism is somewhat unfair. Up until now, that is not what companies retain them to do. They are simply brought in to offer their advice on *how you should job hunt*. When it comes down to their recommendations… they too have their clients rely heavily on networking and contacts.

The Lack of Real Solutions… Is Why We've Created the New McKenzie Scott Job Search System

It is against that backdrop that the McKenzie Scott System was pioneered, refined and developed into something that meets an enormous need in our society. It's the most powerful new development in the world of job hunting that's ever been assembled.

Fortunately, technology and service innovations are making it possible to overcome each and every one of the obstacles mentioned. Just as technology and the Internet have made possible dramatic breakthroughs in dozens of industries, so it can do for most job seekers—at last.

That's because McKenzie Scott has invested years of work in creating software programs, databases, marketing solutions, specialized websites and thousands of links that help solve the problem.

What do all of these do? They put **all the information you need,** *and only the information you need, at your fingertips... if you decide to look for a new job. That includes the openings you need... leads to openings... and people who can connect you to openings.*

What's more, if you are a job seeker today at the professional level, we'll distribute your credentials to targeted recruiters and employers who represent high probability contacts. This means getting you market exposure well beyond what you could do on your own.

At the same time, we recognized that market exposure without having the right story to present to the market... the right resumes ... would not work... just as people also need to have superior interviewing skills.

So, we built first-class writing capabilities and assembled the most experienced personal marketing experts to complement our information and distribution breakthroughs.

The result? A remarkable "interview driven" system that has been designed to slice through the information explosion and give people the resources they need to approach job hunting with more confidence than ever before.

Introducing the McKenzie Scott System... A New Way to Change Jobs

McKenzie Scott has pioneered world-class resources for assisting people seeking a job change. Our experience with tens of thousands of clients has enabled us to continuously develop ways for bringing more speed and convenience to the job hunting process.

In certain respects, our system is similar to well-known diets, medical and other processes for assisting people in improving themselves. While not everyone needs all of our resources, our system must be followed in a specific sequence to maximize its effectiveness. This handbook is your step-by-step guide to using our system and maximizing your market exposure and results.

The Good News—It's Important to Understand the Big Picture, and Realize That Right Now...

There are hundreds of thousands of positions available... through thousands of publications.

There are tens of thousands of positions available... through thousands of recruiters.

There are a million positions available... on employers' websites.

There are hundreds of thousands of jobs emerging... in tens of thousands of growth companies.

There are thousands of positions emerging… in start-ups.

There are at least a million positions soon to be emerging… in other employer organizations.

So why is it so hard for managers, professionals and executives to find new jobs?

We are in the midst of a changing job market and an unprecedented information explosion. You will not make it in this new job market with any reasonable speed… unless you understand it and can take advantage of it. This is where smart personal marketing comes into play today. Understanding today's real job market… and the essential role of marketing… is foreign to most and far removed from their previous ideas about job hunting.

Part 1 of Everyone's Challenge Is…

Finding information they need about openings… leads to openings… and contacts that can connect them to openings. *On their own… how can people expect to find and extract only the 1/1000th of 1% of situations where their credentials should be under consideration?* Using advanced technology is the only way.

Part 2 of Everyone's Challenge Is...

This has to do with how people package themselves, the importance of which has been magnified by our information explosion. To be effective, today people must emphasize only the right things about themselves, and communicate what they can contribute with greater clarity than ever before. Furthermore, to succeed in today's market, they have to communicate through multiple resumes, letters, emails, phone conversations and more.

On their own, how can people realistically expect to do this effectively? Taking advantage of the right professionals... with the right technology resources behind them... is the only efficient way to tackle this.

Part 3 of Everyone's Challenge Is...

Succeeding in today's highly competitive interviewing environment. People are changing jobs more frequently and they are living and working longer. Along with PCs, faxes and the Internet, this has accelerated a 30 to 50 times explosion of resumes. As a result, interviewing is exceedingly competitive.

With this level of competition, *how can people realistically succeed at interviewing and negotiation if they just depend on their natural skills?*

These three challenges are why most people's chances of making a connection with "a good job" are exceedingly small. It's why job hunting takes so long, even when so many jobs are available. It's where our investment in technology and personal marketing resources comes in.

Six Years and a $20 Million Investment... McKenzie Scott's Answer to Each One of These Challenges

McKenzie Scott has created technological and marketing resources to allow you to do the following:

- You can surface, organize and prioritize the totality of all of your experience, achievements, and skills... the information about you that will be most appealing.
- You can have solutions for any liabilities that might restrict you in the eyes of employers and recruiters.
- You can run your job campaign with professionally written resumes and letters... materials that allow you to compete to the maximum your talents will allow.
- From the thousands of industries and different career possibilities... you can surface your realistic options, and know how to alter your marketing appeal to decision makers in new areas.

- From the sea of information out there, you can access technological resources to extract the microscopic portion of what you care about in the market... at the right income level... specific openings, leads to openings... and connections that can introduce you to openings.
- You can get the market exposure you need because of our technological capability for targeting and placing your credentials in small or large quantities with key large employers, growth firms, recruiters and VCs.
- You can use a proven system for interviewing that enables you to: (1) better read interviewers and adapt your behavior; (2) build maximum chemistry; (3) handle difficult questions; and (4) project your best image.
- To help with negotiations, you can use our step-by-step system with words, phrases and sample correspondence for all your negotiating situations.

Besides breakthroughs in technology, we do not use career counselors or a single advisor concept. Each client can draw upon a marketing team... experienced and talented people who are experts on our system and facilitate it, who solve individual problems, formulate custom strategies, and make sure clients know how to use our resources to gain their best competitive advantage.

With This Capability People No Longer Need to Settle for Less Than a Job They Really Enjoy

Having the right job can make you a different person. It can affect your feelings, your mood, your family, your energy and your outlook on life. Unfortunately, when it comes to jobs, most people in the world play it safe. They tend to underestimate themselves and therefore remain in positions which are dull, routine, unchallenging, and that offer little future or excitement. These people have stopped growing... even though most of them have a remarkable reservoir of talents that are untapped.

1 Why Some People Fail in the Job Market—the Job Hunting Dilemmas They Never Solve

Many people fail to confront a number of factors that will impact their success. Here are some that might apply to you and that our service will address. Not all of the following may be questions that require resolution in your case.

#1 Reason Some People Fail... They Don't Go After the Right Job... in the Right Industry

If you are about to make a career move, it will be helpful to keep in mind the following perspective. Each executive career is a journey. At each stop along the way, as you decide on a job, you choose from a number of possible futures. Your selection changes your life, but it also determines all the remaining career choices that will ever become available.

That's why finding the "right" new job is so critical. If you just settle for an "okay" job, chances are you will end up disappointed. "Okay" jobs don't stretch you. They don't require the full use of your skills and knowledge. They don't enable you to develop new skills, don't offer a major increase in income, and fail to make you more marketable. How often have you seen others take jobs with average potential? They took jobs that were just "okay."

This first dilemma can be challenging. However, more high-level people than ever are making career changes. They move from education and government to business, from nonprofit to the private sector and vice-versa, and many change careers within business.

But how do you know which new career options to explore? How do you qualify yourself for a new career? Our service addresses these issues.

When it comes to industry options, there is obviously a world of added opportunity when you are in a growth industry... rather than one that is tired or declining. But how do you know which new options to pursue? And, how do you identify and communicate those unique elements of your experience that would get people in new industries excited about seeing you?

One of the great strengths of our service is surfacing industry options. We also identify the skills, assets and key phrases to communicate in various resumes and letters.

#2 Reason Some People Fail...
They Don't Handle Their Liabilities

This is the second dilemma. Make no mistake about it. Everyone who recruits is looking for liabilities, reasons to rule you out... not in. But, the most common ones include:

- Career may have peaked/or have age concerns
- Lacking blue chip or large firm experience

- Being unemployed
- Leaving a firm that performed poorly
- Having changed jobs too often
- Being seen as too narrow or too generalized
- Closely associated with a firm or industry
- Leaving a short-term position
- Lacking the right education credentials
- Lacking impressive titles/career progression
- Having gaps in your work history
- Lacking line or staff experience
- Lacking experience in the industry you are targeting

Strategies for handling any concerns are important, and we provide solutions for any that may pertain to you.

Last year, through our recruiting subsidiary, Executive Search Online, we surveyed 2,000 executives who found themselves frustrated and still looking for a new job after 12 months. We asked them what they thought was the root cause of their problem... what caused their lack of success. In the statistical summary on the following pages, you can see where they placed the blame.

Essentially, this paints a picture of why they think their searches failed. Of course, hindsight is always easy, but... 96% blamed lack of access to openings, 91% blamed lack of industry options, 87% felt their resume was the problem, and 77% lost out in interviews.

Now the tragedy of this is that all of these issues could have been resolved in advance... saving these executives from an enormous amount of anxiety… and from ***drifting in the market*** for so long. It didn't need to be this way.

But, let's go further down the chart and you'll see *liability issues* that people felt were the cause of their problem. 68% said unemployment gave them a bad image… 65% said age held them back… 62% said that they were too specialized or too generalized.

The real shame of this situation is that *talented people* needlessly put themselves through a lot of despair—undoubtedly costing a lot of time and money.

We've learned that any client's concerns should be addressed up front… and strategies put in place to minimize the impact of any liability. If you fail to do this your entire job hunting effort can be put at risk. The fact is that any good marketer… whether it's Dell Computer, Honda or J & J… knows their products aren't perfect! But they find ways to market them and overcome any shortcomings.

Search Issues

96% Lacked access to right openings
91% Lacked industry options
87% Needed better resume
77% Failed in interviews

Liability Issues

68% Unemployment hurt
65% Age was problem
62% Too specialized
55% Experience in a single industry

47%	Lacked blue chip experience
29%	Changed jobs too often
22%	Titles lacked career progression
20%	Previous firm performed poorly
20%	Reference issues
16%	Left a short term job
15%	Recent jobs were too similar
13%	Had shifted from main field
9%	Was seen as overqualified

#3 Reason Some People Fail... They Use Average Resumes and Rely on Trial & Error

Does your resume go beyond a simple presentation of where you've been and some achievements? Will employers easily see the full value of what you offer? At your level, employers have to see *a lot of value* to make a hiring decision!

Our copywriters focus on creating persuasive and distinctive materials, which capture the very best expression of you.

Once you have your materials, just like a sports contest, it's important to have a game plan... a step-by-step action plan that lays out what should be done, where, when and how. If you just jump into the job market, chances are you will fall victim to lengthy trial-and-error job hunting.

To avoid this, our staff creates a custom marketing plan aimed at developing several interview opportunities in a range of action channels. Over the years, we've learned that a good plan can cut your job hunting time in half; and when you generate a lot of activity, you will feel better and do better.

#4 Reason Some People Fail...
They Aren't Ready for Competitive Interviewing

Interviewing isn't what it used to be, not when there are so many finalists under consideration. We've seen some of the most polished executives in the world disappoint themselves in interviews.

How do you take control of critical interviewing sessions? How do you separate yourself from the others in the final stages? Can you wrap things up without missing a step?

We help you with each of these issues. Our goal is to make sure you are fully equipped and ready to compete with a maximum advantage.

Negotiating, of course, is not just about money and stock options, but the nature of each job and everything that goes with it. Since most of us seldom face this experience, few of us are real experts here. As part of our service you learn our negotiation philosophy. Then, as you encounter negotiation situations, we are there to strategize each stage.

#5 Reason Some People Fail...
They Can't Find Enough Openings

Advertised openings on the Internet can represent opportunity. But how do you find time to track down the best ones? And when you respond, how do you differentiate yourself from hundreds of others?

The overwhelming size and scope of the Internet is intimidating. Navigating it is a hit-or-miss proposition, and its global reach vastly increases competition. It's also easy to be disappointed when you search for good positions. But, we've solved the Internet job hunting problem.

To accomplish this, we've invested millions of dollars in an ***online client information center***. We put everything that's relevant in one easy-to-use place. Essentially, we make it possible to avoid reams of irrelevant information and track down many more of the right opportunities... and in significantly less time. Most important, our information center facilitates access to a significant portion of the published and unpublished markets.

#6 Reason Some People Fail...
They Fail to Maximize Recruiters

Recruiters are an option. But, which ones should be approached? And how? Will your resume command top consideration? And, how do you get a recruiter to present you for a job with real career advancement... not just an "okay" job?

Recruiters account for about 9% of all executive opportunities. With this in mind, as part of our service, we make sure our clients define and blanket this segment of the marketplace. Some of the things we do include distributing your resume electronically to thousands of recruiters who may have interest.

We also supplement electronic distributions with first class mailings. Through our information center, you also are able to review openings with recruiters throughout your search... and submit your credentials accordingly.

#7 Reason Some People Fail...
They Never Maximize Their Networking

Traditional networking can be time-consuming and sometimes demeaning. We believe in networking, but at the executive level, we have a different approach. It is briefly outlined in this handbook in Chapter 14. Approximately 10% of our clients accept new positions which stem from the networking philosophy that is described. Our consulting staff is skilled at creating just the right networking message.

#8 Reason Some People Fail...
They Don't Know How to Use Direct Mail

Done properly, direct mail can produce highly qualified responses—in a far less competitive environment. The key is to have the right targets, use superior materials, and use finely tuned strategies.

We believe in direct mail to CEOs and officers for most job campaigns. While some direct mail to employers is part of our core service, we also make it possible for you to do your own direct mail. You can order custom mailing lists through the interactive segment of our information center, and contact selected employers with your materials.

For senior executives, contacting board members is a viable option. However, do you know what works and what doesn't? Are you aware of the materials required? A lot of finesse is involved. To assist you here, we can give you the benefit of what we have learned... and, if you wish, can handle a number of board member mailings for you.

Highly Marketable or Less Marketable ... Today, People Need to Do the Right Things

If you're highly marketable, you need to make the most of the fine record you've built. And if you are average, or below average in marketability, you need a competitive advantage to make up the difference.

In either case, you need to face up to the fact that without enough market exposure, your chances of winning the "right" job in today's job market are incredibly small. Getting market exposure is what we help people do.

The right market exposure can change your confidence and self-esteem. When your schedule is full of telephone discussions and interviews, your will to succeed will build on itself. That's when people can take control their own career destiny, rather than trusting their future to fate.

Classic Career Situations

Are you a young executive at a career crossroads?

Are you a corporate officer in a bad career position?

Have you had too many jobs?

Have you been too long in one firm or industry?

Are you an entrepreneur returning to the market?

Do you have an age concern?

2 Classic Career Situations That Demand Superior Execution

While each career is unique, there are certain common situations we encounter frequently. If you fall into one of them, this discussion may give you some initial guidance.

Are You a Young Executive at a Career Crossroads?

These executives are typically 28–46 years old, BA/BS or MBA, doing well financially, either highly marketable and confident... or concerned because they have been blocked in middle or upper management for some time.

Many potentially great careers are lost at this critical stage. People in this category seem to be at one of the most important crossroads they will face. Some come to our service from a position of total strength. They are confident and highly marketable, but do not want to settle for what comes to them each month from one or two recruiters.

These executives want to explore *all* their options before they make a move... not just one or two. Here, all elements of our service play a role.

On the other hand, some executives are less confident. They've found themselves blocked for some time. Some fail to discover the importance of broadening out before it's too late. Age is a factor here. They're well aware of the bottleneck at middle and lower upper management.

Some of these people are in situations where they have not attracted attention from top management. Other talented people may be just ahead of them—or they may not be aligned well enough politically.

Often, if they search on their own, they risk making a mistake. Because they value their careers so highly, a bad move at this stage can be tragic and they know it.

The advantage of having an objective appraisal of their marketability and options can be critical. For this reason, the aspect of our service where we uncover assets, skills and options often takes on significance.

If some of these executives don't get control of their careers now, they may lose the advantage of their good beginnings. They need to choose their options properly, stage their careers and plan their futures. Some are not far from falling into mediocrity, or having their marketability decline—which means it is the best it will ever be right now.

Our philosophy is that these people are often wise to consider new environments in smaller and medium-sized companies, and in emerging industries—where they can quickly receive much greater responsibility.

Working in an entrepreneurial environment and combining it with large corporate experience can be an excellent platform for future moves. It may also be time for some to take a calculated risk in trying to make a dramatic move up financially. They are ready to do their boss's job... and perhaps much better!

Executives like this often dabble in the market... answering ads, speaking with a few recruiters. Doing this, they might surface something sooner or later. But, it is almost always only one offer—requiring a one-shot leap of faith.

These executives can get enormous benefit from having us create their action plans—giving them a structured system aimed at developing the right interview opportunities. Good numbers are necessary because we have found that executives have to be realistic about rejections. And, the higher you go, the truer this is.

Are You a Corporate Officer in a Bad Career Position?

The corporate officer—$100K to $750K+... age 36 to 62 ...often at the peak of their marketability. Job is threatened, challenge gone, or been terminated... may be getting some activity, but not the right activity, and not enough of it.

Executives in this position are often unsure about their futures. Normally in control, they sense changes ahead. They fall into two groups. First are the highly marketable who know their options. Second are those skeptical of the future.

A few may begin to be concerned that they have wasted their best career opportunity. Others may be fed up with politics and want out entirely, but are uncertain of just how to do this. Some worry their careers could be lost at this stage.

At higher levels, these people are often concerned about campaigning with dignity. They may also feel that they cannot afford to make another mistake. Their next move often needs to be the last they plan to make, and time may be their greatest enemy.

<u>One key rule of thumb:</u> If you have recently lost your job, don't be seduced by a false sense of security and ride out the severance. Unemployment is a liability... and over time, you will dig yourself a deeper and deeper hole.

Remember that the perception among employers is, good people don't last long in the market. For this reason, executives need to get control of their plans... and fast. They need a campaign approach, or risk facing a bleak future.

On the positive side, unemployment can be an advantage if it is seized as an opportunity to take a sober, careful look at all options. Some, of course, have such high marketability that they may be faced with the burden of choice—*but not know "how" to choose or "what" to choose*. Here again, an important thing we do is to help them identify, prioritize and take control of their options.

There is a tendency for all executives to have an exaggerated view of their marketability. They need to gain much wider exposure than they realize.

Surprisingly, our surveys indicate that 50% of executives who make a move on their own... begin thinking it was a mistake in six months. Why? Many take the first thing that comes along. This is why a lot of activity is essential.

Of course, for corporate officers at senior levels, the resumes and letters we professionally create have even greater importance. They make or break the success of their campaigns. For many, we reshape their entire backgrounds to qualify them for new industries.

Without clear thinking and superior writing, many of these executives would drift in the marketplace. As they get some good opportunities, our ability to help them negotiate their best package is vital. Today's world of executive arrangements is very complex.

(As an aside, we have found that even the most senior executives often have a misunderstanding of technology firms. A fear may exist because they are not technical and feel they would not be a good fit. This is not the case. It's not your technical orientation. It's all about your skills and abilities.)

Will You Be Viewed as Having Had Too Many Jobs?

Often, a client will come to us after several bad moves. Emotionally, they may be confused, and despite talent, they are doubting themselves. Frequently, they are in a poor state of mind.

Typically, this is where an executive is confused, concerned, or wondering if there is any hope. Is the problem with them, or are they a victim of circumstances? "Where in the world do I go from here?" You need to realize there is a root cause for what happened and come to grips with it.

These executives often have a lack of focus in terms of industry direction. They have begun to lose hope for the future. Some recognize that their careers are in shambles. Some feel lonely and vulnerable.

If they examine their previous campaigns, they will usually recognize that bad moves in the past were made because they didn't approach the search professionally.

Their past problems *were most likely not with them, but in how they made their changes*. These mistakes need to be avoided. Historically, some of these people have been trapped in a pattern of action and reaction. Some have overreacted against past problems by then taking the first thing that came along. In the past, faced with this type of situation, the short-term *solution* they saw turned out to be their long-term *problem*. The key point: They need to break their pattern now.

For many, the key to their success is in our ability to get them connected to enough openings. Then, with our strategic help during interviews and negotiations, they need to accept the right situation and stay with it.

Will You Be Viewed as Having Been Too Long in One Firm or Industry?

Some clients retain us to do a search, but have not fully committed to a change. Often, things are uncertain and they are restless and want to see what's out there, beyond their narrow experiences.

These people may have earnings that are quite high... or modest... because of their long stay. They do not know what they are worth and may never have looked before. For this reason, the part of our service that expands their true marketability is paramount.

Given an honest choice, these people probably would not leave their current employer if they did not believe they were missing out on the things other people have—more income and challenge, recognition and future.

Unless their lethargy is really shaken, they will probably spend the best years of their lives with indecision. Action for these people may come too late to be meaningful. Often, they are inwardly looking to be encouraged to stay where they are, while also feeling a burning desire to achieve more than is humanly possible. In their own eyes, they are in danger of labeling themselves as *"less than a real success."*

Sometimes, lack of confidence in their marketability may have been fostered by years of plodding in anonymity. They may have been taken for granted for so long that their identity melded with their firm. The reality is that they are often quite marketable.

Most of the time, these people are unaware of what's really out there. The convenience of our service is most critical in these cases.

Not only are they unaware of what's out there, but employers will be ignorant of their value, because they have never prepared a resume that qualifies them for new directions. And whenever there's a problem of ignorance, the solution is communication.

The weight of these campaigns falls on their ability to build an appropriate bridge, both through their resumes and communication in general. Their old resume often telegraphs their major liability—their one company or one industry experience—and has restricted their activity.

We get concerned that in this category, the longer they wait, the more difficult it is. Executives in this situation need to understand that they have already stayed too long, and they need to make a decision to cut their losses. In all likelihood, if they do not move soon, they should not change at all.

Are You a Former Entrepreneur Facing a Return to the Market?

These executives are seasoned enough to recognize that certain employers will be hesitant to hire someone who has owned a business. They know there will be concerns about whether they may go back in their own business, whether they can be a team player, and whether they can accept corporate structure.

Talented as they may be, former entrepreneurs face special challenges. Many are identified with a narrow industry segment. They are concerned about their credibility outside that niche, and want to stay in part of their previous industry.

Of course, some want, or need by virtue of non-compete agreements, to seek out positions in entirely different industries. However, they are unsure of how to go about identifying where they would fit. Some, having been successful financially, now want to be in a business which has an explicit mission involving services that will enrich people's lives.

This is a critical move for them, one they have not made before *at their current level*. They know the importance of doing it right. They are practical, down-to-earth realists, and know they need to approach employers the way they would like to be approached.

For entrepreneurs to have credibility, they must have concrete "selling propositions." These should be things they can relate to, as well as "industry hooks" based on facts and the realities of the marketplace, not just vague generalities.

Entrepreneurs are seldom short on achievements. However, where they need the most help is developing powerful written presentations which make them credible over a broader spectrum. Another critical need for entrepreneurs is to have us work closely with them throughout all interviews and negotiations. This is because most have never had to go through a search at their level before.

Are You Someone for Whom Age Might Prove a Major Liability?

Many clients seek us out because they have doubts about competing. Their age may be a barrier for the responsibility their pride and ego commands. Regrettably, if they believe age is the barrier, and remain unhappily employed elsewhere, this mental obstacle effectively blocks their putting forth the required energy to make the right move.

Some people use age as an excuse for not searching. Their confidence may be on the wane, and they may not want to admit it, but despite their experience, they don't really know how to search at their level. Dealing with perceptions about age is like any other task. You progress if you take action.

As you might suspect, action starts with their beliefs about themselves and what's possible. As they work with our evaluations, barriers fall as we surface their marketable skills.

They come to understand that their marketability can be enhanced through communication of all the skills, know-how and personal strengths they possess. If they can contribute, age is irrelevant. People tend to forget: Employers think about themselves, their problems and their own challenges. Now, there is no question that age will eliminate people from opportunities. That's why our aggressiveness is a valued service feature. They need to put the numbers on their side, and now is the time.

Our specialists identify all the credible industry hooks they possess—broadening the functions they can fill, as well as the industries they can target with confidence. Obviously, superior materials are essential.

Then, our technology enables their credentials to be put into play for a significant portion of all suitable openings during the time they are searching.

Just as it is true that age will eliminate some options, it is also true that young management teams look for veteran talent to add balance.

Today, people in their late 40s and 50s are connecting with fast-growing companies, especially in new industries where experience is in demand. Last year, we also helped many clients in their early 60s.

Just for the record, a common thread bound the following people: Commodore Vanderbilt, Socrates, Pasteur, Voltaire, Newton, Talleyrand, Thomas Jefferson, Galileo, Martha Graham, Armand Hammer, Grandma Moses, Adolph Zuckor, Ronald Reagan, Coco Chanel, Dr. Benjamin Spock, Winston Churchill and George Burns. Each made his or her major accomplishments after becoming a "senior citizen." So, again, don't put any limits on your own thinking!

Getting Into Our Service—Stage 1...
Getting You Prepared—the Right Way

Most people never take the time to properly prepare. Then weeks turn into months. Soon, they have to start over and prepare the right way. The next five chapters (3–7) review how we get you prepared.

Understanding and expanding your marketability

- ❑ Organizing your lifetime of experiences
- ❑ Pinpointing transferable skills
- ❑ Providing solutions to any liabilities

Reviewing your career options and goals

Reviewing your industry options

Putting in place a communications plan... what to say... and not say

Professional writing of several resumes

Our clients typically find this very enlightening. Many have said that coming to grips with all of these issues builds confidence and self-esteem.

Our customer satisfaction rate with what we present is over 99.3%. Fewer than 1 in every 290 clients fails to agree that our thinking is insightful, on target and enormously helpful. We guarantee our clients' full satisfaction with what we present.

The successful, most efficient job search follows a classic business principle: An organized and experienced team will invariably outperform the inexperienced individual working in his spare time.

One of the major myths about job hunting is that you can always get an equal or better job. That's simply not true anymore. It depends on your marketability, and this has to do with you... and the market.

Now it's not so easy to determine how marketable you are. But, we can statistically figure out where you stand, and what changes need to be made to enhance your marketability. It's a valuable reality check... a helpful step that may change your entire perspective.

3 *Understanding Your Marketability Is a Must... But Expanding It Is Also Essential*

The new job market is so competitive you'll need to do more than just present your background. Don't trap yourself by thinking, "This is simply who I am, where I've been and what I've done." Many people fail because they never surface and communicate everything that is marketable about themselves... and they never build their appeal beyond obvious factual credentials. Now, thanks to our resources, our clients can avoid this problem.

The McKenzie Scott CHAMP Organizes a Lifetime of Experiences

It is important to review this section before you complete our *Career History and Marketability Profile* (CHAMP). However, it is vital for another reason. Whether you are a young attorney or a company president, there is probably much more to your story than meets the eye.

Our CHAMP is a remarkable instrument that will reveal insights which our staff can use to expand your marketability and help build your appeal. Along with information from our discussions and through our other profiles, our staff develops your marketing plan and all written materials. Thousands of people have said that completing our CHAMP is very insightful. Now, besides your experience, let's first discuss what else may be marketable about you.

We'll Surface All Your Assets and Skills

We can almost guarantee you that you cannot identify 50% of your own assets, simply because you're too close to your own situation. As we surface everything that's marketable about you, chances are we'll identify 15 to 25 skills which, if selectively communicated, can make the difference.

Each year, 10% of the clients who come to us have settled for less, simply because they've never been able to communicate their real skills. One client was earning a $65,000 base after almost 20 years. Three years later, she is earning $180,000. Another executive came to us at $125,000. Three years later, he is a CEO at many times that amount. The key in both situations was that we marketed their true assets.

Now, if you are like most people, you can increase your chances through a very simple rule. It has been said time and again by psychologists, spiritual leaders and coaches that the most restrictive limits you face are those you put on yourself. So, don't put any limits on your thinking.

We'll Make Sure You Know How to Market Your Knowledge and Personality

Do you have knowledge of a job, a product, a process, or a market... from work, hobbies, alumni relationships, research, consultants, or suppliers? If so, it may be marketable.

Personality, of course, is just a word for that mysterious combination of traits that either attracts us to someone, or, on the other hand, leaves us unimpressed. More employment decisions are based on personality and chemistry than any other factor. For example: *"He's certainly professional and quick-thinking. I like him, and better yet, I trust him. He'll get along with our team. I need to get him into this firm."*

The perception of your personality has to do with your interests and enthusiasm. How many employers hire people primarily because they showed great interest? *The answer is, a lot—at all levels!*

If You Have Leadership Qualities, We Decide How to Market Them

If there is one quality you want to communicate, it is leadership ability. Experts say that leaders possess and communicate real convictions—strong feelings and principles that have grown with them over time.

Leadership is also attributed to those who create an image of operating at the far edge of the frontier... into new products and solutions. We tend to think of leaders as those who have the vision and talent to develop new things.

Another skill common to most leaders is their ability to recruit or assemble a team which they motivate to peak levels of achievement. Other attributes people ascribe to leaders are that they are creative, intuitive and passionate, and they project integrity, trust and boldness. Image, attitude, appearance and presence all play a role.

We'll Identify Your Critical Transferable Skills That Show Your True Versatility

Identifying transferable skills is critical (for example, organizing, group presentation skills, problem solving and so on). Today, employers clearly place a premium on men and women who are versatile. Executives in highest demand are those who can move from challenge to challenge, handling assignments that draw upon different skills.

Naturally, your experience can also be reviewed according to various "functions" that apply to most businesses, such as sales, production, accounting, marketing and human resources. All areas in which you have knowledge must be identified. At the same time, you need to think of your experience in terms of "action verbs" that describe what you did, and then translate those activities into achievements, i.e., *controlled, wrote, reshaped,* etc.

The more ways you can describe your experience, the more you will qualify for jobs in many industries. All organizations are involved in similar functions.

Our Marketability Comparison Report—First We'll Measure Your Marketability... Then We'll Improve It

Job hunting is demanding in many respects. Particularly frustrating is the fact that it is one of the most competitive efforts you will undertake. Unfortunately, you never get a chance to know who your competition is! But, employers and recruiters will be viewing you in terms of your competition. Their job is to measure how you stack up on key qualities... how you compare to other qualified candidates.

Each month, more than 10,000 candidates complete our marketability evaluation profile. They grade themselves on 225 assets and skills which are being sought by the country's leading recruiting firms.

Through our proprietary software, we are able to provide a ***detailed statistical analysis***... one which compares you to 2,000 other professionals seeking positions within the last month, in the same income range. This gives us a detailed numerical reading on just how marketable you are. Our report will indicate the experiences, achievements and qualities your competitors possess, and how you stack up.

Our professionals can then suggest strategies and a course of action designed to further increase your marketability... and give you a competitive advantage. For example, we routinely identify which elements of your experience and strengths need to be emphasized, those areas where you excel, and others where you need to communicate differently.

The bottom line is that through our marketability comparison, all of your communications can be adjusted to consider the qualifications of those you will be competing against.

As a result, your resumes, letters and emails can be more persuasive... and your phone presentations, interviews and negotiations can also be far more effective.

Who's Your Competition?

Our recruiting subsidiary, Executive Search Online, supplies us with many statistics about the job market and current executives who are looking for new jobs. During the month of July 2003 they had 3,000 job seekers register with them, completing an extensive profile, after responding to a national advertisement placed in *The Wall Street Journal*. The following statistics will provide you with a revealing glimpse of who your typical executive level competitor is.

Time in the Market So Far

Average weeks	27

Current/Most Recent Income

Mean income	$125-150K
Under $100K	37.2%
Over $200K	12.3%

Boards Served On

None	56.8%
1-2	32.1%
3 or more	11.1%

Education

BA/BS degree	57.9%
MBA/MS degree	43.1%
PhD	2.8%
JD/LLB	2.6%
Some or no college	6.7%

Unemployment

Employed	64.8%
Unemployed or soon to be	35.2%

Length of Unemployment

Average weeks	15.5

People Managed

1-20	36.3%
21-100	34.8%
101-500	17.9%
over 500	10.1%

Budgets Managed

None	8.7%
$1-5M	19.8%
$6-25M	21.5%
$26-100M	25.1%
Over $100M	13.0%

Reasons for Searching

Better growth opportunity 42.7%
More excitement/challenge 39.6%
Increased income 37.2%
Unemployed or about to be 34.8%
Expanded responsibility 27.1%
More enjoyable work 25.1%
Greater authority/status 17.8%
Prefer new location 13.5%
Getting back to mainstream 13.1%
Prefer new industry 12.3%
Greater stability/security 12.3%
Prefer new career field 11.8%
Greater people contact 10.9%
More independence 9.0%
Better political environment 8.3%

Areas of Experience With Major Achievements

Worked with top mgmt. 85%
Handled many projects 78%
Formulated action plans 70%
Built self-sustaining teams 67%
Improved sales / profits 64%
Been in top management 62%
Had P & L responsibility 62%
Improved productivity 61%
Handled strategic planning 59%
Turned around poor attitudes 58%
Experienced at cost control 53%
Personally brought in revenues .. 53%
Negotiated major deals 52%
Substantial staff experience 50%
Managed a lot of people 48%
Initiated sweeping changes 47%
Managed large budgets 47%
Designed efficient systems 46%
Developed strategic alliances 46%
Managed complex operations 45%
Chaired multifunctional teams ... 44%
Reorganized and revitalized 43%
Managed rapid growth 43%
Simplified complex problems 42%
Sat on key committees 42%
Been at division officer level 42%
Been at corporate officer level ... 42%
Instincts for what will sell 42%
Excellent with technical matters 39%
Skilled negotiator 39%
Large admin. responsibilities 38%
Turned around operations 38%
Multi market experience 38%
Highly social 38%
Re-engineered processes 37%
Directed startup 37%
Substantial line experience 35%
Sophisticated, cultured 34%
Excellent recruiter 33%
Started prototype operations 28%
Experienced with multi plants ... 23%
Joint venture experience 22%
Flair for putting on events 22%
Served on nonprofit boards 21%

Areas of Experience With Major Achievements (continued)

Works a 70-hour+ week 21%
Acquired operations 20%
Strong at consumer selling 19%
Large material responsibilities ... 18%
Chaired civic organizations 18%
Served on civic boards 17%
Served on corporate boards 16%
Published author of articles 13%
Negotiated acquisitions 13%
Opened new plants 11%
Skilled at governmental affairs .. 11%
Procured major funds, grants 8%

Personal Qualities–Phrases That Previous Bosses Would Use to Describe the Candidate

Very dependable, loyal 88%
Highly self-motivated 79%
High achiever 78%
Ambitious 73%
Good-natured / personable 72%
Well respected, esteemed 72%
Exceptional team player 71%
Very persistent 71%
Exceptional people skills 69%
Decisive 69%
Drive "out-of-box" thinking 67%
Very positive, very upbeat 65%
Sense of humor 65%
Assertive 65%
Quick thinking 65%
Hands on / shirt sleeve 62%
Highly resourceful 62%
Strong written communicator 62%
Natural leader 62%
Strong verbal communicator 61%
Wins cooperation at all levels 61%
Great motivator 61%
Highly versatile 60%
Strong analytically 59%
Conceptual 59%
Highly competitive 58%
Excellent executive image 57%
Very persuasive 56%
Strong personal presence 55%
Outgoing 55%
Strong group communicator 54%
Highly innovative 54%
Tactician / strategic thinker 52%
Highly organized 50%
Highly creative 50%
Risk taker, entrepreneurial 50%
Exceptional listener 47%
Excellent trainer 46%
Excellent long-range planner 46%
Superior writing skills 45%
Visionary 45%
Strong administratively 43%
Strong at corporate selling 43%
Instincts for what will sell 42%
Excellent with technical matters 39%
Skilled negotiator 39%

Highly social 38%
Sophisticated, cultured 34%
Excellent recruiter 33%
Flair for putting on events 22%
Perfectionist 19%
Strong at consumer selling 19%
Skilled at governmental affairs .. 11%

Financial Strength & Goals

Have a good credit rating 82%
Next move is very critical 59%
Would consider work at home ... 57%
Prefer to move ASAP 53%
Have reserves to last 4-6 months 47%
Seek minimum 10-15% more 43%
Have reserves to last 7-12 months 37%
Have reserves to last 13+ months 34%
Seek stock options / equity 38%
Prefer to move within 6 months . 27%
Seek minimum 25%+ more 25%
Not urgent - just exploring 8%
Would work on full commission .. 8%

Investment / Equity Interest

@ $25K 20%
$26k-$50K 13%
$51k-$100K 7%
$101k-$200K 5%
$201k-$500K+ 1%

Organizations Where People Have Marketable Experience

With national firms 78%
With public companies 67%
With firms at $1 billion+ 67%
With market leaders 66%
With Fortune 1000 firms 59%
With service firms 58%
With firms under $100 million .. 56%
With start-ups 48%
With manufacturing firms 45%
With growth companies 44%
With firms at $100M - $250M ... 41%
With firms at $501M - $1B 40%
With high-tech firms 39%
With firms at $251M - $500M ... 37%
With blue chip firms 36%
With small consulting firms 33%
With Internet/e-commerce firms 25%
Worked outside North America . 23%
With large consulting firms 21%
Owned business, sales $1mil+ ... 21%
With IPOs 20%
With non-profits 17%
With major accounting firms 8%

How Some McKenzie Scott Clients View An Analysis of Their Marketability

"Your marketability evaluation made a lot of sense and clarified what I needed to emphasize in all my communications. We were really able to raise the bar when it came to communicating my skills."

"My whole purpose in engaging McKenzie Scott was to make an industry change out of retail. The marketability evaluation zeroed in on my skills and qualities that could be of value to many types of organizations. We devoted a major portion of my resume to communicating them properly."

"Knowing your marketability, and knowing it has valid statistics behind it that covers all the bases, has to be enlightening for any executive."

"A good starting point is to really be honest with yourself. Put your assets, liabilities and needs under a microscope. I feel the key to job hunting is just like marketing a product. You have to really know your product before you start selling it. Otherwise, you can waste months and months of time."

4 *We Review the Full Range of Your Career-Change Possibilities & Help Set Your Position Goals*

Many executives have successfully embarked upon entirely new careers. But, doing this on your own isn't so easy. We help each client decide on specific position goals. Then, we pinpoint subsets of words for emphasis... the skills that employers associate with the job being sought. Along with our recommendations on industries that should be explored, we refer to this as properly "positioning" each of our clients.

It may surprise you, but a lot of people pursue the wrong job titles. However, once we surface all their transferable skills, we're often able to reposition them, and for more advancement than they previously thought was possible. Regardless of your most recent position, you are "one of a kind" and should be presented accordingly.

Many people have learned that their career fields can change dramatically in the course of a decade. Fields that once offered great opportunity can be viewed as financially confining with limited growth possibilities. Does print advertising offer the same career possibilities as it did a decade ago? Does selling in the steel industry? Does being a doctor who is a general practitioner? Career fields not only change, they change at a much faster pace than most people realize.

Experience has proven that if you take a narrow view of yourself, you could be making a major mistake. If you see yourself as a specialist, you may believe you are locked into a given career. Or, you may feel you have few options because you are a generalist.

Believe it or not, there are 22,000 different job titles in use today, but 95% of all professionals fall within one of several hundred career specialties.

As part of our service, we jointly decide on the career goals that are right for you at this time. If you are a candidate for a major career change, we'll examine the range of new job options that might be appropriate to consider.

Many people want an industry change.
But, few know how to make it happen.

One of our specialties is helping people qualify for positions in new industries. 60% of our clients change industries. Over 90% say they would not have been able to do it without our resources.

5 *Our Staff Will Help Uncover Your Most Exciting Industry Options*

To help our clients, we start by having tens of thousands of professionals complete our Industry Characteristic Profile each quarter. This enables people to tell us the specific characteristics of industries where they've worked.

Then, when a person becomes our client, we have special software which identifies the range of industries, including emerging, growth and traditional industries... that have similar characteristics to their own.

Today, people must be prepared to market themselves with sufficient skill so that they are attractive to employers in many industries.

The reality is that executives of all ages are making moves into emerging industries. Many find such choices allow them to have greater income and more challenge. Here, we'll share some basics we have learned from the many executives we have helped to change industries.

Our exhaustive analysis will surface your assets. Then we match them against a range of opportunity areas. Transition to a new industry is easier than it used to be. Historically, people have overrated the barriers and underrated their abilities to move into new areas.

If You're Like Most People, You Should Look Into Growth Industries

As a rule, we identify a range of possibilities that people may not have uncovered—on their own. Of course, we also consider traditional areas and large firms. Ultimately, clients select their own goals.

We tend to favor growth industries. Why? Because a fast-growing firm generally means higher pay, faster promotions and more valuable stock options—giving people a chance of accumulating some wealth and job satisfaction.

This remains true even with the current accounting controversy over the expensing of options.

Growth companies are usually driven by shareholder value. Every employee receives more options each year. Of course, there are restrictions regarding tenure with the company. But if a person joins a growth company, they have the potential at any age for compensation in stock options that can go far beyond their salary.

Our Philosophy About Making It Easier for You to Change Industries

We track growth industries and companies by constantly updating our knowledge through relationships and information sharing. Our research department also continually reviews hundreds of media, newsletters and online sources. Any mention of a growth industry goes into our growth file.

From there, we isolate characteristics of each industry and match them with characteristics of industries where our clients have previous experience. We refer to this as having an "industry hook."

Projecting some form of an industry hook is the next best thing to having industry experience. Our goal is to compile your best possibilities, and we group them three ways: *Close industry hooks...easy possibilities; medium industry hooks... next best; far reach or stretch industry hooks.*

The more you appear to know about an industry, the easier it is to generate interviews. Conversely, the harder it is to demonstrate knowledge of an industry, the less likely you will move into it. If you are short on information about an industry, the easiest way to acquire knowledge is through trade publications. They make it easy to talk about new products, specific firms and the major industry challenges.

A client was a marketing executive with Philip Morris and she joined a cosmetics firm. Why? Their methods of marketing are similar.

Another client was the EVP of a computer firm, and was recruited to become president of a firm that makes power packs. Why? The industries have similarities in manufacturing.

A defense executive became CEO of a firm selling high-tech services to military contractors. Why? The key was the CEO's market knowledge.

Another way to get this knowledge is to talk with people in the industry. You can also use our *information center* to surface information on virtually any trade association and its key executives.

Turnaround Opportunities Can Work

Troubled industries can have a lot to offer. Executives who have worked for firms under pressure can be invaluable contributors. Tough lessons learned in competitive battles can put you in demand.

As you review industries, you might also remember that while glamorous high-tech and service businesses receive 90% of all publicity, many people will find far more opportunities in industries that are considered low-tech.

Obviously, you don't want to overlook your leverage power... the added benefits you may bring by virtue of your contacts or knowledge. You may be able to bring a team with you that helped you "turn around" a similar situation. Perhaps you control major accounts that would help business. Or, you may have cut millions from overhead and can do it again.

Emphasizing Your Versatility

Another consideration can be your versatility. The fact is, nearly every capable person can work in a different function that is broader, narrower, or in some way associated with a past position. Here are some examples to reinforce this point:

A GM from Mattel became the marketing VP for a consumer firm in the cosmetics industry.

An executive went from the Labor Department to president of a pharmaceutical firm.

A lawyer from a steel company became EVP of an engineering company.

Be sure to communicate the scope of your knowledge and potential. Sales executives, for instance, often know quite a bit about marketing, purchasing and distribution. Manufacturing professionals often know a great deal about administration, logistics, the control function and general management. A controller may have a grasp of every aspect of a business.

When discussing the requirements for a position, it will be important to distinguish between arbitrary requirements and those that really relate to results. These include degrees, titles and industry experience.

The Ability to Produce Results... Your Core Selling Proposition

The final hiring decision usually has little to do with specifications. If you can present yourself convincingly as being able to produce results, you will most likely get the job. We have thousands of examples. If you believe you can produce direct results, lay claim to it. Don't seek a lower level than you should, or rule yourself out because you have never done a job before.

You have achieved certain things in a specific way, using your unique combination of skills, knowledge and personal traits. If you know they can be applied to a prospective employer's challenges, make that clear... and use stories.

The McKenzie Scott Industry Characteristic Profile

As mentioned, we have tens of thousands of professionals complete our Industry Characteristic Profile quarterly. This checklist form contains hundreds of "descriptors." It lets clients tell us about the industries where they've worked.

For example, an executive who had been with the fast food giant "McDonald's" would probably check that his industry was characterized by such things as *heavy national advertising, strong brand development focus* and that it was *manpower intensive*.

On the other hand, an executive who had been with Time Warner's cable television group would probably describe his industry as being *capital intensive*, *subject to government regulation* and other descriptors.

When you become our client, you will complete our Industry Characteristic Profile. Then, we will utilize our software to identify other industries that have similar characteristics to your own.

How Some McKenzie Scott Clients View Industry Change

"I had been in manufacturing for 20 years here in Pittsburgh. The key to your helping me was your thorough way of analyzing my whole career history. Working with your staff, we came up with completely different presentations based upon my skills. The whole search took about 15 weeks but I am extremely excited about the firm I have joined."

"As I look back on my purchasing career, I agree with you that being in the right industry can have a major impact on your career and financial progress. I had worked for two tire companies, most recently Firestone, and only wish that I had made an earlier effort to break into a new area."

"I've been an educator for most of my life. Without some marketing experts to talk to, I think most executives would have a hard time pinpointing their industry options. Your staff enlightened me to a dramatic extent. I have now shifted from a career in nonprofit and education to the business world."

Few people compare finding a new job to a politician running for election. But, just as in politics, planning your messages can make an enormous difference.

A "communications plan" not only makes good sense... it's essential. It sets a theme for your personal PR plan.

Jointly, we'll develop the vital phrases and stories that will set you apart... and which you'll use in all your communications.

6 *Our Communications Plan Will Create Added Strength for Everything You Communicate About Yourself*

We will develop a way to convey "the real you" with precise phrases that will form your "communication strategy." (Please realize that your "tickets" alone ...advanced degrees, titles, etc.... won't necessarily motivate someone to hire you.)

With the approach to expanding your marketability just described, we will jointly set the stage to build appeal beyond your basic credentials.

To appreciate your need for a communication strategy, consider the "platform" of a candidate for the Presidency. It anticipates questions on issues and formulates well-thought-out position statements to guide the candidate's answers.

Now, when any of us recruit, we have a concept in mind. In the final analysis, we hire others for the skills and abilities that certain key descriptive phrases imply. So, it's important to select those that set you apart.

For example, you may have *"operated effectively under pressure,"* or you may *"know how to introduce change smoothly."* From hundreds of phrases we will isolate the appropriate ones which will set you apart.

To expand your marketability, you must develop stories to create maximum interest. Without stories, most people will forget what you say in a matter of minutes.

The McKenzie Scott "SOAR Concept" Will Make You More Memorable

To make your points memorable, we use a method for creating interesting stories. SOAR is an acronym that stands for Situation, Opportunities, Actions and Results. It's a process for describing your experience.

We all like good stories and remember them. SOAR represents a compelling way to present information about your history.

In these stories, you need to indicate positive things you did to help organizations and how you took on extra tasks. Describe how you helped your management team meet their goals, and the results they achieved. If appropriate, show how you demonstrated a special skill or a personal quality.

Develop SOAR stories that cover situations where you can demonstrate the value of fresh thinking as a means to improve productivity, or show that you have solved a variety of problems in diverse areas.

Employers need to feel that you are the answer to one of their problems. If you can show them how you met or exceeded the needs in other environments, they may conclude that you can do the same for them.

The idea is to create stories that demonstrate the benefits you bring. If you successfully managed the integration of two teams following a merger, and the new business gained market share—by all means, say so.

Millions of Job Campaigns Stall Because People Don't Have Solutions for Their Liabilities

As part of our communications strategy for you, we will also recommend solutions to any concerns. Regardless of what it may be... a bad reference, the fact that you are perceived as too specialized, or perhaps a concern about gaps in your employment, we will suggest how these should be addressed. The idea is to plan in advance how to deal with anything that might restrict you in the eyes of employers.

Our philosophy is to take each concern, one by one, and decide how it can be handled in all the forms of communications you will be using. This includes your resumes, letters and emails... as well as phone discussions, interviews and negotiations.

There is an enormous amount of misinformation about resumes. Articles in many newspapers and several dozen books contain advice that has little to do with reality.

This has created a problem for many people. Their concept of resumes is way out of tune with what works today.

In this market, it's simply not enough to have an average or even slightly better than average resume. And, to make the most of each situation, you will want to use multiple resumes—for different purposes. Does any major marketer use just one advertisement?

You need nothing less than great materials. Nothing is more critical to your success.

7 *We'll Do Three Superior Resumes to Let You Compete at Your Best*

We've invested countless hours in testing thousands of different materials and developing empirical evidence that is a very clear indication as to what works... and what doesn't.

We believe in creating several different professionally written resumes to help ensure that our clients can maximize their opportunities in different situations. And, the resumes we write are geared toward reducing interviewing pressure by pre-selling our clients as much as possible.

Unfortunately, when we look for a job, we're reduced to how we look on paper. 95% of resumes are inadequate. They are average in appearance, disclose liabilities, are uninteresting, and are rarely about what people can contribute.

Since the early 1990s, the growth in the use of PCs, fax machines, the Internet and email has resulted in firms receiving *50 times* more resumes than in the past. *Staffing Industry* sources have indicated that 30,000,000 resumes are being circulated. Many employers have embraced resume-scanning software and shifted to new ways of selection.

In this environment, our management, as a result of tracking thousands of searches, has developed a more effective approach—one which utilizes several types of resumes, all targeted for different applications. This has afforded our clients a significant edge.

Solution Resumes Are the Key

Resumes must be a solution to each career situation, packaging all your key skills and experiences. The style, tone and every word must be crafted to capture the best expression of what you have to offer.

Many executives have told us that they have mailed over 5,000 resumes prepared by a mailing service and received nothing in return. Yet, a strategic placement of 1,000 of our resumes, highly targeted by industry, produced significant activity and several offers. What's the difference?

We've invested countless hours in testing thousands of resumes. When you have an "A" resume it's not just two times more effective than a "B" resume—*it's more like 100 times more effective*. But, it simply isn't easy to prepare an "A" resume. First you have to know the market. Then, it takes hours and hours to study someone's situation, compare them to their competition and to then create a highly superior document. For our professionals this is a full day of work.

Resumes also need to be written with an eye toward reducing interviewing pressure by pre-selling you as much as possible. The ideal reaction on the receiving end should be, *"Paul, I have the feeling you can really help."*

Your "Pure Gold" Resume—A Universal Resume

This is the first resume we do for all clients. The most essential resume you need is a universal resume—a unique one-page document that will be your introductory resume.

Most people mistakenly believe that they need to tell their whole story in their initial resume. The reality is that you get better results when your initial resume is interesting, with a feeling of action—but short! You want your phone to ring.

This resume will be suitable for key word scanning, with short paragraphs, and both easy to read and compelling. From a content standpoint, it will start with a clear job title positioning statement which reflects the real job titles that employers are seeking to fill, and for which you want to be considered.

Your "Internet" Resume—An Electronic Resume

This is the second resume we do for all clients. Few people understand the issues when they email or post their resume online, and it is surprising how few devote any thought to the way their resumes appear at the receiving end of an email transmission. This resume will be shorter. When you are online, less is more. All you want is a response.

Your "Quick-Response" Resume—Needs No Cover Letter

This is the third resume we do for all our clients. Because much of job hunting is a game of numbers and timing, you have to have a resume which makes it easy for you to respond quickly to certain emerging situations you come across. After all, time is the enemy. You've got to make it as easy for yourself as possible.

For each of our clients, we professionally create this resume. It positions the text on the right-hand side of the page so that you can write handwritten notes and dispatch a resume without a cover letter. Our clients tell us that executives have responded well to their written notes which cited news they noticed on our information center.

Your "Interview" Resume—Revealing Added Details

An interview resume is designed to be a persuasive summary of your experiences—one which intentionally reveals more about you. It is for leaving behind at interviews, once you have made a strong impression—and when it is clear that employers want to know more about what you can contribute. People at all levels can benefit from having this resume.

The "Platinum" Resume—Your CEO Biography

The CEO biography is an extremely powerful document. It is recommended *only* for those who are competing for a CEO or COO job, or who expect to be hired with the approval of the president or CEO.

Over the years, we've seen many situations where an executive expected an offer but saw interest drift away. Decision makers often "pass on" a resume to the top executive or board members, to get consensus. The offer becomes dependent on a "thumbs up" on the resume presentation.

Our CEO bios are three to five pages, and written from a third-party perspective. They are long stories and rich in detail. They are also highly favored by top recruiters because it makes their jobs easier. To do a bio takes top writing talent and a lot of experience in knowing what works and what doesn't. Even then, it takes our professionals two days to create, edit and finalize all materials *and get them approved by our own Creative Review Board.*

The McKenzie Scott Collection of Outstanding Marketing Letters

Good letters will always customize your appeal to each audience. Our clients receive our comprehensive guide entitled, "*Writing Outstanding Job Search Letters.*" This includes an extensive sampling of letters that have proven effective for others, and which are very easy to copy or adapt. More than 75 samples are supplied on disk, and cover all the situations you are likely to encounter. Some clients have us professionally draft these same letters for them. The portfolio we create includes 12 letters for the following occasions:

For responding to openings
For contacting recruiters
For contacting venture capitalists
For responding to spot opportunities
For direct mail contact with employers
For sponsored direct mail to employers
For contacting directors of associations

For networking associates and friends
For networking alumni from your university
For networking influential people
For setting up potential references
For following up your interviews

Getting Into Our Service—Stage 2...
Your Marketing Action Plan for Getting Interviews

Our next section has to do with getting you into the market with maximum market exposure.

- ❑ Understanding today's job market
- ❑ Your step-by-step track
- ❑ Helping you access far more openings
- ❑ Why we blanket the recruiter market
- ❑ Venture capitalists and where they fit
- ❑ Direct mail to officers and board members
- ❑ Contacting growth and change-driven firms
- ❑ Our approach to executive networking

Our customer satisfaction rate with the presentation of our ideas and solutions relative to everything above is 99.3%. When we present your custom marketing plan, we guarantee your satisfaction. Fewer than 1 in every 288 clients fails to feel completely comfortable with our ideas, approaches and action plan. The next seven chapters (8–14) will review our philosophy on the subject matters above.

Perhaps the most common myth about job hunting is that when you need a job, you can simply write a resume and start your search.

But, if you're 40 and earning $100,000+, you're about to market a product with millions of dollars of earnings capacity. That much value deserves your best thinking and planning.

Besides, job hunting is a numbers game. Making a lot of contacts is your surest way to guarantee that you will generate a lot of the right interviews. Why take a chance and proceed without a well-targeted and very aggressive plan?

8 *Just Like IBM and P & G… To Avoid Trial & Error, You Need to Use a Marketing Plan*

Most people fail to take enough actions. They just proceed by trial and error and this sets their search back many months.

Having a strategic plan will save you time and money. More important, the marketing action plan will serve as the step-by-step blueprint for your entire search. It will enable you to take balanced actions through a range of channels for getting interviews.

Over the years, there have been many occasions when we have seen equally talented executives produce varying results. One will struggle while the other moves with surprising speed and confidence. Those who move with speed usually have the benefit of a game plan.

We refer to this as having a marketing action plan, a step-by-step track to guide your efforts. In today's competitive arena most people will never get enough interviews with a hit-or-miss approach, or if they depend on one action source— e.g., searching for openings or depending on resume mailings. Taking a narrow approach trusts too much to fate.

A McKenzie Scott Team Will Create Your Marketing Plan

Normally, we design it around a 10 to 16 week timetable, depending upon the situation. We also address what you should do week by week. It is a complete track to follow.

For many executives, job hunting is largely a matter of having the numbers on your side. For this reason, our action plans are often targeted to produce 15 to 25 positive responses that might lead to interview opportunities. This is necessary because the goal is to have several offers maturing at the same time, and you have to be realistic about rejections.

As part of a balanced marketing plan, we never expect too much from any action channel. Rather, our goal is to get a variety of situations through each of the channels for producing interviews. Balance is the key.

A good plan can cut job hunting time in half and sometimes save tens of thousands of dollars. It also helps people produce better results. We have found that when executives generate a lot of activity in a concentrated time period, they feel better and do better. Much better!

How McKenzie Scott Clients View the Importance of Marketing Plans

"I expect a lot from any investment. While many aspects of what you did were impressive, I felt your giving me a clear path to follow was the cornerstone to everything else."

"The marketing plan you prepared was rich with detail. No stone was left unturned. When you start out with this kind of structure, you avoid wasting huge amounts of time."

"I have joined Hewlett Packard as a national sales manager. Your marketing plan summarized the entire process for me, in basic and easy to follow terms. Your written report was long, but it ended up being my reference bible throughout."

Knowing and understanding what to do… isn't the same thing as doing it.

Your goal should be to develop 2 to 4 attractive interviews from each of our 7 major ways for getting interviews… which are covered in the next section.

Then, you can be realistic about rejections and still have a chance at developing several good offers mature at the same time.

Understanding the "Real Job Market" and the 7 Ways Our Clients Connect to the Job Market and Develop the Interviews They Need

The U.S. job market can be broken into six segments. Four represent released openings which can now be reviewed through the Internet—*if you know how to find them*. Collectively, they represent the one-half of the market referred to as *the published job market*. The private or *unpublished job market* makes up the other 50%.

Employer websites

This market was not accessible until a few years ago, but 94% of major corporations now hire this way. Every day, more employers are listing jobs this way. Why? Recruiting is expensive, and this is the affordable way to recruit. Some major employers now do "all their hiring" this way.

Professional job boards

Also referred to as e'cruiters, some specialize by industry and some by level. Through our information center you can now access openings directly from hundreds of these sources. However, waiting for a job to come your way from a resume posting will be a real long shot.

Recruiters

In the past, openings available through recruiters could not be reviewed. Today, thousands of recruiters list jobs on their websites. Again, through our information center you can access these openings.

Newspapers & magazines

This market is rapidly declining, but it is more accessible than ever. We make available, instantly at the touch of a button, openings in 3,000 newspapers and over 2,100 trade magazines.

Expanding companies

Historically, identifying growth firms took weeks of library work. Now, through our information center we enable you to rapidly access them throughout the U.S. Focusing some effort here can bring many people unusual opportunity.

The market through contacts

To access this market, you traditionally had to use personal connections or network associates. Now, we'll equip you with information resources that will allow you to go after these jobs in other ways. The key is using databases and other information, and being able to sort and sift to the right targets. Then, you can go directly to the organizations who do not release their openings through other means.

When you look for a new job today, it's critical to run a search that lets you take advantage of opportunities in each of the six market segments, especially those areas we call less competitive.

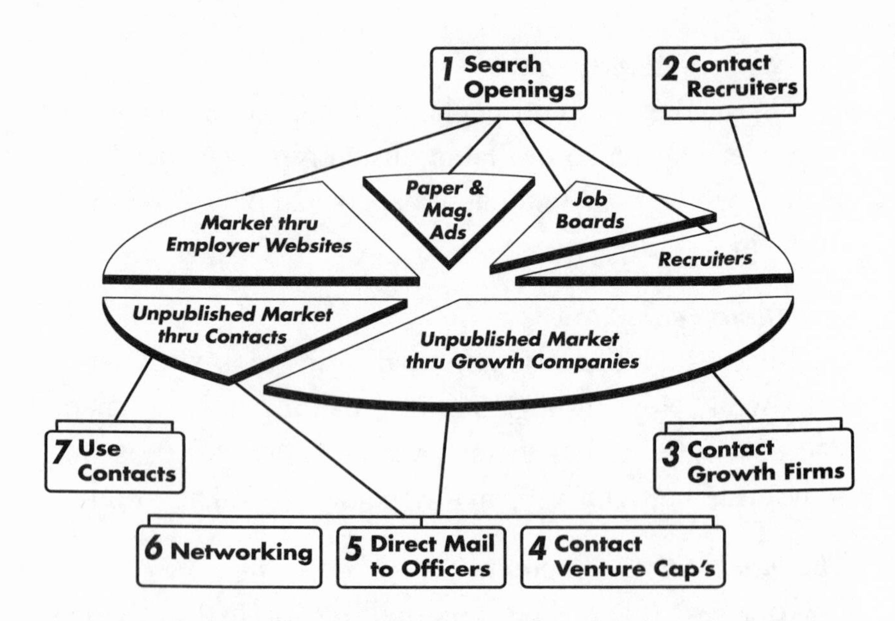

The graphic above illustrates the real job market and the seven ways we help our clients get interviews. Access to the market is available through *The McKenzie Scott Information Center,* which is privately available to all clients. Here's a brief overview.

(1) Searching and responding to openings

You can search openings in each of the first four segments of the published job market. In most situations you can search by your preferred locations of interest and the level of situation that interests you. At any moment in time, more than 1,700,000 openings are on our system. Here, you can also use our Advertised Market Supersearch Technology... an extraordinary selection tool that took us one year of programming to develop and refine.

(2) Contacting recruiters

Besides giving you access to thousands of recruiters and reviewing recruiter openings on our information center, we will also distribute your universal resume to up to 200 local recruiters via 1st class mail... and up to 3,000 nationally via email. We can also distribute your materials to 1,000 premier recruiters who use resume scanning systems and who want to receive the resumes of our clients.

(3) Contacting growth firms

We maintain a file of 7,000-10,000 firms who are among the fastest growing organizations in the U.S. To get you started we will distribute your resume to approximately 200 of these firms in your local area. In addition, through our interactive service, you can order a mailing list of additional firms, and do a larger mailing on your own. To attack this market further, you can identify fast growing firms through events you can identify on our information center.

(4) Contacting venture capitalists

We track the 2,600 major venture capitalists and will place your resume with up to 200 of these firms if it is appropriate. Again, you can use our interactive capability to develop a mailing list for a national search, or we can also do that for you. Furthermore, we can isolate firms receiving VC financing in various stages, and in many cases directly connect you to their openings that may be of interest.

(5) Direct mail to officers and board members

Our fifth way for helping you generate interviews includes using direct mail to employers to attack both parts of the unpublished job market. To get your search off to a fast start, we automatically place your credentials with 200 key employers in your area.

If you wish, we can also handle custom direct mail efforts involving contact with 1,000, 2,000 or 3,000 firms. In addition, you can also use our interactive ordering system to request an employer mailing list according to the criteria you establish. Here, we maintain dozens of premier databases to allow clients to assemble custom mailing lists within 24 to 48 hours.

(6) Executive networking

Our sixth way for helping you generate interviews is to use our advanced methods for executive networking. Once again, you will be able to use our technology to identify key executives to target.

(7) Maximizing your personal contacts

Our seventh way for helping you generate interviews is to help you take advantage of any contacts you may have that can be of help in your search. Here, besides professionally writing the materials you should provide, we give you access to our information center to identify lost contacts, influential alumni who might be of assistance and much more.

Let's Contrast the McKenzie Scott Approach With Traditional Methods

How People Get Their New Positions

Because they are unable to generate activity in all six segments of the job market, people are forced to depend on contacts and networking. Our clients get much broader market exposure, which reflects in the way that they end up getting their new positions.

How People Succeed—Traditional Methods

3 % from contacting employers directly
3 % through answering ads or online openings
9 % through agencies or executive recruiters
59 % from existing contacts and direct referrals
23 % from other networking efforts &
3 % by miscellaneous means (placing ads, through trade associations, alumni centers, committee searches, computer match, etc.)

How People Succeed—McKenzie Scott

34 % from contacting employers directly
24 % through answering ads or online openings
23 % through agencies or executive recruiters
9 % from existing contacts and direct referrals
9 % from other networking efforts &
1 % by miscellaneous means (placing ads, through trade associations, alumni centers, committee searches, computer match, etc.)

Average Length of Active Searches

	Traditional Methods	***McKenzie Scott***
Scientific	16.7	6.8 months
General management	13.7	6.6 months
Legal / consulting	12.6	5.4 months
Human resources	11.9	5.2 months
Accounting / finance	11.1	4.1 months
Misc. staff positions	10.9	4.0 months
Operations	9.9	3.9 months
Office management	9.4	3.9 months
Marketing / sales / RR	8.8	3.5 months
Engineering & related	7.3	3.3 months
Information systems	7.1	3.1 months

Obviously, these statistics are general data, and you need to be cautious in relating them to your own situation. In the case of McKenzie Scott clients, length of campaigns can be expected to vary widely with the level of income people are seeking, and their transferable skills and other credentials.

In addition, those seeking major industry changes take longer than people seeking straightforward advancement *(e.g. a marketing director in consumer products who wants to become a VP marketing).*

However, results will vary the most with the aggressiveness that people give their searches. Listed on the next page are statistics for people who implemented our marketing plans, and who made extensive use of our resources.

Length of McKenzie Scott Aggressive Clients

	Average	*Aggressive*
Scientific	6.8	...... 4.1 months
General management	6.6	...... 3.9 months
Legal / consulting	5.4	...... 3.8 months
Human resources	5.2	...... 3.8 months
Accounting / finance	4.1	...... 3.7 months
Misc. staff positions	4.0	...... 3.4 months
Operations	3.9	...... 3.3 months
Office management	3.9	...... 3.2 months
Marketing / sales / RR	3.5	...... 3.2 months
Engineering & related	3.3	...... 3.1 months
Information systems	3.1	...... 3.1 months

Obviously, campaigns for more senior executives take longer. In addition, people in mainstream fields *(accounting, finance, sales, marketing, operations, etc.)* can expect to move with far greater speed, while specialists such as chemists, patent attorneys, mechanical engineers and many others can expect to have more challenging campaigns.

Getting 80 to 85% Market Exposure... Instead of the Typical 2 to 3%

With all the resources at our clients' disposal, they can be much more aggressive. Because of developments in technology, they can look for market exposure equal to 80-85% of what's out there for them during the time they are in the market, instead of the 2-3% typically achieved.

With most of our best clients, the length of their search is far less important than the market exposure they get. What counts is the quantity and quality of interviews and offers that can be surfaced during a reasonable period. We rarely advise them to take the first thing that comes along, as they need to keep focused on getting the career opportunity that's best for both the short and long term.

Some Further Comments on Why You Can't Depend on Old Approaches and Networking

As mentioned, using traditional methods, most people (82%) get their jobs through networking and direct referrals. You need to look behind that figure to understand its importance. What's really significant is: the low percentage of jobs people got from contacting employers directly; the low percentage they got from answering ads in papers or online; and the low percentage they got from executive recruiters.

Using traditional methods, only 15% got their new positions through these sources, compared to 75% among our clients—a difference of 5 times! Why?

They could not identify and contact growth firms or employers who were their highest probability targets. They could not contact enough recruiters or find enough of the advertised positions particularly well suited for them. When they did, their resumes and letters did not set them apart.

As a result, they surfaced fewer opportunities, and took a lot longer doing it. Our clients have a huge advantage because of our technology and ability to help them surface interviews in every segment of the market.

The added comparisons about interview opportunities surfaced (not positions accepted) illustrate the difference even more dramatically.

% who surfaced interview opportunities through...	***Traditional***	***McKS***
Growth firms	2%	92%
Employers fitting profile	1%	92%
Recruiters	27%	96%
Surfaced through news items	5%	73%
Advertised openings	27%	91%
Openings posted on websites	7%	83%

The implications are obvious.

One of the keys... if you want to win an ideal job instead of an "okay" job...

You'll need to surface a number of good opportunities at the same time ...which means you need many times more opportunities to consider... so you need to generate them from all segments of the job market.

A myth that is common to job seekers who are not succeeding is that they can't find enough openings. This is directly related to the way they search the market.

Remember the last time you looked for a job? Now, through our information center, you can access 50 to 100 times more openings.

Select openings from hundreds of job boards... thousands of recruiters... tens of thousands of employer websites... and 5,100 papers and magazines.

9 Through Our Online Client Information Center You Can Access More Openings Than Ever Before

Through our remarkable private information center, you will be able to connect to virtually all published openings in the U.S. This portion of the market now accounts for more than 1.7 million new openings each month... through job boards, newspapers, trade magazines and other sources.

Even with our capability, you will want to follow through on the broader plan outlined in this book. That's because published openings attract hundreds of responses... and responding to them *is the most highly competitive form of seeking your next position.*

On their own, most of your competition will answer ads without giving any strategic thought to how to gain a competitive advantage. Their resumes will be average in appearance and most will fail to highlight how they can fill a position. Rarely interesting, they will be much more likely to be lost among the overwhelming numbers of resume.

But, the fact remains this will be highly competitive. So with this in mind, what is our best advice here? For most people, we recommend that time spent in responding to openings should be given 10% of your total effort.

Obviously, you will want to respond to positions which sound on target for you. However, our experience has proven that responding to situations a step above... and a step below... is worthwhile.

Here are some guidelines for expanding the opportunities. A firm that advertises a job for a CFO might be willing to hire an executive to start as a VP and move up within a year. After all, it isn't so much the title being sought as the skills and talent. That's an example of *downgrading a situation*.

By the same token, a company advertising for a Plant Manager might be persuaded to hire a VP of Manufacturing if such a move would provide added capabilities. That's called *upgrading a situation*.

Openings in one area can also be used as signals for openings in other areas of the firm. If you see a firm hiring a lot of salespeople, that's almost a sure indicator that they are also hiring in several other areas.

By the way, many firms ask you to submit your earnings. At higher levels, you get better results if you indicate a range or objective, rather than stating your earnings. This subject is better dealt with in interviews.

Answering the Perfect Opening

Did you ever see an opening and feel "*that's me exactly*"? When this happens be sure to respond by sending a tailored letter that is targeted at the requirements for the position.

Then, if you have not heard anything after two weeks, follow up. Employers give a big edge to people who demonstrate they really want to be with their firm.

You may also wish to try some innovative approaches. Try getting added information beyond what was in the ad, and use this information in your response. Demonstrating industry knowledge works better than anything else.

Internet Privacy Issues You Need to Be Aware Of

The number of resumes posted on the Internet is forecasted at 35 million in 2004, with rapid growth in the years thereafter. This is a development with vast implications for the hiring process. Unfortunately, many executives reveal details, seemingly insignificant, which they later regret.

This is especially troublesome because of resume scanning and key word retrieval processes. Once scanned, your resume may be available historically to subscribers of e'cruiting services for decades.

One of your concerns should relate to people who might view your resume. These services have been growing rapidly, and certain executives have had their resumes exposed to casual friends, former subordinates and others and have been caught totally by surprise.

This is one more reason we prepare our clients' resumes with great attention to detail.

How McKenzie Scott Clients View the Internet

"I had used the Internet for two months and was quite frustrated. One of the biggest values your service brings is your information center. You put everything useful on the Internet in one place, without the 99% that isn't useful."

"There is a lot written about using the Internet. But the fact remains that without your information center, it's difficult to navigate, and hard to find appropriate openings."

"What your information center did was make it a lot easier, by bringing everything to one place. For executives in more popular occupations like sales, marketing, finance, operations, etc., what you have done is excellent."

"I was surprised to find the number of openings that I did. I was a candidate for jobs at about 150K, either as a Sr. Controller or as a CFO in smaller organizations. One of them turned into a very good position which I accepted."

"I wanted a step up from my situation with General Mills. The search took longer than expected, but I landed a position as a Division President. The openings through your information center were very helpful."

10 Why We Blanket the Recruiter Market for All Our Clients

The chance of an executive recruiter filling a job that is right for you, at the moment you contact them, is remarkably small. Blanketing this segment of the market is the only way to go.

We market the electronic resume we prepare to up to 3,000 recruiters who want to receive the resumes of our clients. We also send 200 copies out via first class mail to local recruiters of interest. Through our information center, you also are able to review and respond to openings that thousands of recruiters now post online. With our system, getting the most out of recruiters is not a one-shot effort... it's a continuing effort.

Whether they are called search firms or headhunters, all recruiters work for employers. They screen candidates, filling jobs at $80,000 to $1,000,000 and up.

Typically, they are retained for exclusive searches at fees averaging 33% of compensation. To distinguish themselves, they are also referred to as "retained recruiters." Contingency recruiters are also active up to $150,000, receiving a commission only when a placement is made. Another growing category is the temporary executive recruiter. They earn fees when employers hire professionals on an interim basis.

To develop any level of good activity with recruiters, you'll need absolutely superior materials.

You'll also need to go after every legitimate recruiting target. That's why we cover this part of the market so thoroughly for every client.

We believe you should give yourself exposure to a maximum number of recruiters. While your percentage response will be low, you can often create instant activity.

The number of executive jobs with recruiters is sizeable, but comprises only 7 to 9% of the market. While 8,000 firms claim to be active, fewer than a dozen dominate the upper-end business. However, many fine smaller firms specialize by industry or discipline, and play an important role. Importantly, the best recruiters play a role in helping management set up position specifications.

Recruiters have a preference for achievers, people who make strong first impressions and who are employed. Being visible in your industry can be a major key with recruiters. Being in a hot field or industry can really help. If you are in your 30s or 40s, you should always develop and maintain relationships with recruiters.

The manner in which recruiters find candidates has shifted rather dramatically due to the Internet's impact. Half of all assignments are now filled by candidates who are identified through massive databases of scanned resumes.

The other 50% of recruiter assignments are filled through traditional methods. A small percentage are filled through ads placed online or in print media, while a larger percentage is filled through networking referrals. Some assignments are filled by firms targeting individuals working for competitors.

Remember, recruiters are "assignment-oriented." They will focus on filling their active contracts. And you will simply be placed in their files.

You should also know that parallel processing is a recruiting practice where a candidate is introduced to more than one client of a recruiting firm. However, many recruiters say they consider this practice unethical, thus restricting your opportunities as a candidate. This is just one more reason why you need to be in touch with a lot of recruiters.

When you communicate with recruiters, never be negative about your current employer and never appear desperate. Many large firms are contacted by as many as 200 job seekers each day. They may not get in touch with you until *months* after they get your resume.

What to Expect From Resume Distributions to Recruiters

We have a capability that can quickly launch a search. Once clients approve their e'resume, we distribute it via email. It is then up to them to continue to build interest. Here are some guidelines. People with recognizable "tickets" do best (for example, well-known schools, degrees, blue chip company affiliations, good titles, etc.).

This distribution can be effective for those in popular occupational fields (e.g., sales, accounting, finance, IT or IS, manufacturing or service operations and other fields where there is a sizeable demand).

It is far less effective for those in narrow or low demand specialties (e.g., a patent attorney, city manager, technical writer, blood chemist, etc.) or for those making a career change (e.g., an educator moving into business).

Also, as a person goes up the pyramid, there are fewer jobs available, so the response for the less senior professional is generally the best.

Stated another way, those who position themselves with lofty titles and high income, as well as those without recognizable "tickets" or who are in narrow demand areas, should not expect too much here. It's a low percentage game. That is why compensating with greater numbers is required.

We also place resumes with recruiters in hard copy form. For executives interested in the best regional or national positions, we can also do a distribution by first class mail to our blue chip list of 1,000 recruiters. This is directed at firms that initially select resumes for scanning into their database. As they receive search assignments, they then retrieve resumes by key words.

Our clients receive responses from this type of mailing over many weeks and months. Note: A second electronic or hard copy distribution to the same list three to four months later produces about 80% of the initial response.

Obviously, there can be no assurances of success, since the effectiveness of distribution depends on the demand for an individual's field and background. There is no way to accurately predict response, since everyone has his or her own unique identity.

Accessing Recruiter Openings Through Our Information Center

Several thousand recruiters post their openings online. When you enter our information center, you can select the state in which you have an interest and the level of openings. Then you can instantly review job listings.

You will be most popular with recruiters if you will explore attractive situations but are not openly unhappy with your current employer. Because timing is critical, "luck" can play a significant role.

Recruiters are important for most executives. To recap, however, keep in mind that the chance of a recruiter filling a job that is right for you, at the moment you contact them, is remarkably small. Their quantity of assignments can also fluctuate widely with the state of the U.S. economy.

If you are not well known in your field, it is important to blanket this segment of the market. This includes electronic and first class resume distributions, but also personal registrations on the websites of leading recruiters, and responses to current openings which they post online.

How Some McKenzie Scott Clients View Recruiters

"I worked every angle of your system, but my activity with recruiters was for high quality jobs. Employers who spend money for large recruiting fees value their positions more. When they pay $60,000 to get a job filled, you can also be sure that the job you accept will have some room for negotiation."

"I got a lot from your recruiter distributions. I had 11 interviews with search firms in New York."

"Recruiters won't produce much for you if you want to change fields. At first, I wanted to make a dramatic shift. Then, we adjusted my materials to keep me in my specialty, and the results were entirely different."

"Recruiters response was slow, but over time what we did resulted in several good opportunities becoming available to me. It's pretty much like you said, the way to use your system is to get a few good things going through each action channel, and not to expect too much from any of them."

11 For Certain Executives Venture Capitalists Can Bring Unique Opportunities

Are you a candidate for executive positions with startups or emerging companies? If so, we will want your credentials placed with serious venture capital players... perhaps hundreds of them. On a national scale, there are approximately 2,600 leading VC and LBO firms that we track.

A surprising number of firms have assumed an active role in hiring for both start-ups and developing firms in which they have an ongoing investment.

Clients who generate the most interest are normally executives who are candidates for "C" level positions (COO, CTO, etc.) or those who can fill a role as head of a line function (VP Sales, etc.).

If you have qualifications that would interest these firms, we will electronically distribute your resume to local VCs. If you are a strong candidate for using this action channel, we can also do this nationally. Those who do best here are primarily in their 30s and 40s. Typically, they have been with well known firms and have advanced degrees.

We also make it easy for you to get your credentials in front of VC firms on your own. Through our information center, you can quickly get information on appropriate firms to contact.

How Some McKenzie Scott Clients View Contacting VCs

"I have accepted a position that came through contacting a venture capitalist in Atlanta. My background is in biochemistry and I had been a sales executive with Novartis. I could not be more pleased. I am 53 years old. I did have several things emerge, but all related to my previous industry experience and my MBA and Ph.D. My new position is president—COO of a firm with $10 million in initial financing."

"I am 32 years old, have a BS from Northwestern and an MBA from Chicago. Most recently, I had been with a major consulting firm for five years and engaged McKenzie Scott for only one goal. I wanted to make the shift from staff work as a consultant to a line position. Raising a family, I also wanted much less travel. I had a lot of response from venture capitalists, even in the slower economy. However, while I have landed an excellent position, my starting guaranteed package is $175,000... $50,000 less than my package last year. My stock option package is where the opportunity is, and offers me the upside I wanted."

12 *Direct Mail to Officers and Board Members Can Be Powerful... or a Disaster!*

This can be the fastest way to produce interviews. But, you will need precisely the right targets, outstanding resumes and letters, and strategic followup. Here are our most important criteria.

You have probably seen ads for mailing services with many testimonials and strong success claims. Unfortunately, many executives have purchased such services, sending out up to 10,000 mailings, with no results! These services don't work, because the firms send out five-line cover letters attached to historical resumes. They simply don't qualify people for new industries.

On the other hand... if carefully targeted at decision makers in industries for which your materials have built a strong candidacy, direct mail can be very productive.

And, putting together a mailing list through our information center is easier to do than ever before. There you can get connected to... or order... virtually anything you might need. Keep in mind the following: Direct mail is an extremely low percentage game, one that requires superior materials, focused targets and well-thought-out strategies.

Why does direct mail work? Well, every day we all receive direct mail. Now, however bad that junk mail looks, the ones you see again and again are working; otherwise, the senders wouldn't be wasting money repeating the process.

Historically, a primary rule in direct mail is that long copy is the name of the game, because that's what it takes to motivate all of us to action from *unasked for correspondence*.

Here's an example. Let's assume your local lawn mower shop wants you to come in and see a new product they're carrying. Assume that you and your next door neighbor are both out cutting your lawns on a hot day. However, your lawn mower keeps stopping, and finally breaks down.

Then, the mail carrier arrives at both residences with mail that tells you all about a new lawn mower. It gives a long explanation of why it's superior to everything.

Now, chances are your neighbor will look at the mailing piece for about two seconds and toss it, wondering how anyone could ever read all the material. Obviously, he isn't in the market for a lawn mower. On the other hand, because the mailing piece has reached you at the right time, you are apt to read it carefully, and perhaps make a purchase!

Now, your position, relative to using direct mail, is really quite similar. Your interest is in reaching the right person who might be in the market for someone like you right now. No one else counts.

I asked a friend of mine, a CEO of a high tech company, "What would you do if you had to look for a job?" His response was, *"Well, besides exhausting my contacts and covering recruiters, I'd get a lot of resumes to board members who might view me as a possibility. It works with my board. They know our problems and refer talent."*

Another friend, a VP of Marketing at a Fortune 500 company, put it another way. He said, *"I look at resumes that cross my desk. If something matches my needs at the moment, I usually respond directly. It's a matter of timing."*

A third associate, the head of HR at a Fortune 500 company, sent me the following comment when I was updating this book. His comment was, *"I would highly recommend direct mail. Third-party letters can be especially effective if the right person is writing for you. Just prepare a letter they approve for their signature. Make it easy for them to assist."*

Who to Contact

To make this easy, you need to take advantage of the interactive capability of our information center. There, by using simple order forms, you will be able to take advantage of dozens of databases which we maintain. They can save you immense amounts of time and let you quickly launch either small or large direct mail efforts.

When you compile your list, you'll need each person's correct title, spelling of their name and address. Since most reference sources are 15-20% out-of-date (*including the best)*, if it is an important target, call for correct information.

Now, you must recognize that a very low percentage of employers will need someone like you the day your material arrives. For example, if you were looking for a CFO position, *since those jobs turn over only once every three years*, this means the week your mailing arrives might be "perfect"... but only once in every 156 weeks, if it gets to the right person.

For executives, from 3 to 6 positive responses, sometimes up to 10, typically are generated from 1,000 mailings. Obviously, your success will depend on a host of personal and market factors at the time. Of course, if you had five very good situations to explore, you might not need anything else.

Unlike responding to openings or contacting recruiters, direct mail often produces highly qualified leads in a non-competitive situation. After all, they will have read about you, and want to see you for what your material represents. They will either have a position... or they may be thinking about creating a position.

A key point to remember is that when responses are received, you need to be sure to make the most of them. Never be interviewed on the phone and never rule anything out. You can always use the responses to upgrade within the same firm or to network.

How McKenzie Scott Helps With Direct Mail to Officers

As mentioned, we initially distribute your resume to key local corporations. Our goal is simply to expedite some coverage of the obvious possibilities.

We can also process larger mailings to 1,000, 2,000 or 3,000 employers, all sent at once. Targets are selected from many dozens of databases which the firm maintains.

This can be recommended in those select cases where senior executives can move in many industries. For people such as HR executives, CFOs and General Counsels, large mailings can be appropriate.

Contacting Board Members

We can also identify board members of public firms that we might approach. Or, you can do the same thing by ordering the information you want through our information center.

When we present a candidate to board members, it has to be done in a fashion consistent with the dignity and importance of this level of communication.

Custom letters are mailed under our letterhead on a limited basis every week, for a period of up to 16 weeks. For each contact, we typically bind the custom cover letter with the universal resume and the CEO biography. This enables board members to have both a thumbnail sketch, and an extensive recitation of our client's credentials and abilities in their CEO biography. This presentation is similar to a briefing book that a member would receive prior to a board meeting.

How Some McKenzie Scott Clients View Direct Mail

"I live in Ohio and was not in a position to move. Because of this, your marketing plan had greater emphasis on custom mailings, running down spot opportunities and networking. As part of the strategy I sent out hundreds of 2-page custom letters over a 12-week period. The search took 17 weeks."

"Your mailings went out to 1,000 companies in Dallas. Response was low, but after six weeks the mailings yielded several good situations, and eventually two good offers."

"You did several thousand mailings for me in foods and pharmaceuticals. Results have continued for months. My new position is a divisional COO for Pfizer."

"Mailings were more important for me because I did not want to rely on my contacts. The search took six months. A total of 6,000 mailings went out under the names of three close friends who are senior executives. During the search I had three attractive offers."

"I had tried direct mail on my own and with another firm, but the results were awful. This time your creative work made all the difference. It's the key to everything you do."

13 *Every Job Seeker Needs to Contact Growth and Change Driven Firms... on a Custom Basis*

Through our information center we make it easy for you to identify change-driven firms. You are also equipped with our quick-response resume... to make it easier to bring your credentials to their attention.

We often refer to this portion of your search as looking for "Spot or Emerging Opportunities." Every day, events occur in thousands of firms that lead managers to search for new people. These events are reported in trade magazines, newsletters, newspapers and online media.

What are the events? They are announcements of higher sales, expansion plans, acquisitions, new products and other news that signal opportunity. You want to identify these *change-driven firms*, and it's easy to do with our information center. Often they are hiring across the board.

Firms with problems can also be of interest. Reorganizations involve shifts in executive ranks. They often spell opportunity for those at the next level, and changes ripple down through the firm. Problems often imply that executives haven't been performing well, or the company needs new capabilities. For executives, the CEO or a board member will be the logical person to contact. HR executives will also know of openings. SVPs of functions are an alternative.

Many employers undergoing change are smaller and faster growing firms, who are less constrained by hiring traditions. In the case of growth companies, most will be looking for individuals with the best natural ability and the enthusiasm and willingness to work at an extraordinary pace. Assuming you have marketable talents, a message which makes clear how you can contribute is likely to stimulate interest.

How Some McKenzie Scott Clients Made This Strategy Work

A financial executive read that a troubled manufacturer was divesting a division to raise cash. He called the new president. Four weeks later, he became the CFO.

A product manager read that a local firm had been acquired. He wrote to express interest. Twelve weeks later, he was VP-Marketing, U.S.A.

A general manager read that a major investment was being made near his home. He contacted the CEO and in one month was offered a senior position.

An administrator of a major university hospital, with 15 years in her field, read about a medical equipment firm. She soon started in a position with 20% higher income.

A sales executive achieved his objective of running U.S. marketing for a Japanese camera manufacturer. It all came about from an article in a trade magazine.

Networking Doesn't Need to Be Slow and Demeaning... You Can Do It Right

There's nothing like personal contacts; however, the people who depend on them too much will be in for a long search.

There is always a long-shot possibility that business acquaintances may be able to offer you the right position. Chances are, however, that few will be able to offer what you want. Usually, the best you can hope for is to have them refer you to others who might need someone like you.

Now, random networking can work at lower income levels. But, at $100,000+ it can be a time-consuming way to find a job. Instead, focus your networking on industries which have characteristics that make you a good match.

Networking, of course, is a continuous pyramiding strategy... one where you capitalize on one name to gain an interview with another. For example, *"In my meeting with Mr. X, he suggested it might be of value if we got together."*

Seeking *"informational interviews"* is the most popular networking approach. Here, you wish to encourage executives to share with you some information about their industry, trends and challenges, which recruiters are most active in the industry, and so on. These discussions must be kept brief and you need to have your list of questions prepared. As a rule, executives do better when they have researched a firm and use the *"feedback approach"* to networking. This means asking for feedback on ideas that may benefit the firm.

Be sure to use our information center to find executives to target. They can be in your industry or new industries, but they should be influential people. Consider looking for those who have been featured or quoted in articles, which makes an introduction easy and natural.

Our information center can also help you track down lost contacts, uncover successful alumni and others. Executive Directors of associations have many "lines" into their industries. Editors of business magazines and newsletters may also have an inside track on the needs of specific organizations.

Don't forget those you already know and can contact. Remember, discovering a talent enables people you know to do a favor for the person they refer you to. We all have influential friends... golfing partners, politicians, lawyers, investment bankers and social acquaintances... who know others who could be looking for key executives. All they need to do is handwrite a short note and forward your material.

Networking Through References—The Story of Mark

Mark was a VP who wanted to become a CFO. We helped make Mark aware of the power of his references. When Mark heard his company was to be sold, he felt his salary was $20,000 less than it should be.

Did his boss feel bad about paying him less than he was worth? Absolutely! Could Mark ask him to act as his first reference, and would he raise him to the level he wanted, in return for his staying for the last two months? Definitely.

Now, the boss had a friend in an accounting firm. Mark asked his boss if he would approach his friend as a second reference. Together, they had lunch. The accountant was happy to be a second reference. In the same way, Mark developed a third reference, his own brother-in-law.

When he launched a campaign, he had a good interview with the president of a small paper company. A conservative man, he asked for three references. Mark immediately recontacted his references, so they were ready. After his boss had given him a glowing reference, the president mentioned that he was still uncertain.

When the second reference was called (the boss's friend), he told the president that in the right situation Mark could help save him $1 million in taxes, and control costs. He had repositioned Mark as a broader-based financial executive.

Next, Mark's third reference supported the others and added a few points. The day after the last reference check, he got a call from the president, and guess what? His message was, *"Mark, what will it take to get you?"* He ended up as CFO at a much higher income.

Most of the time, important references will be the people you reported to in the past, the person you currently report to or their superiors, and on rare occasions, the people who once worked for you. Choose the highest level reference, as long as you get an enthusiastic endorsement, and avoid people who don't communicate well.

Which References to Select

References you select should know your achievements and have no hesitation in making strong statements. What they say is very important, but the enthusiasm and conviction they project is more important. Let them know that you have high regard for them and their opinions, and they will want to do their very best.

Don't forget that good references will know only part of your background. Make sure that they learn the full story. Here's an example. A woman who worked for me left to complete her MBA. She was competent, had a quiet manner, but could be forceful. When she started interviewing, she brought me up-to-date. She called to tell me that after an interview with a firm she liked, she felt they had some concerns about her quiet nature.

Armed with that information, I was ready when I was called by her potential boss. Before the question was asked, I mentioned that sometimes people could be deceived by this woman's quiet nature, but that she could be very assertive. The person responded that I had put to rest his one concern.

References can be your best sources of referrals. Leave each person a half-dozen resumes. Reassure them that you won't use them too many times. After calling them, send a brief note that shows your appreciation and summarize a few positive things they can say about you. You can even make a list of questions that employers might ask and suggest answers for them.

By the way, let references know as soon as you have used their names, and ask them to let you know when they have been contacted. Employers will sometimes ask them for the name of someone else who is familiar with you.

How Some McKenzie Scott Clients View Networking

"I had never felt comfortable, as I didn't like asking for help. This time I sent out my CEO bio to 150 people. The response was high and more than 10% gave me leads."

"I wanted to be in the high-end furniture business. Using your materials, I worked my connections. It took six weeks for my first offer. A second came 10 days later."

"McKenzie Scott did a lot for me, but what really helped the most was learning how to use my Rolodex here in New York. Your materials were excellent and my contacts led to a job as executive director of a major nonprofit."

If You Are Employed, When Is the Right Time to Launch Your Search?

Based on our experience with tens of thousands of professional searches, we can offer some wisdom on this subject. Many people concern themselves about the job market. But, what makes national news about the market, will have little to do with the reception many professionals and executives receive in the marketplace.

For example, surprising as it may seem, in good economies or bad, every year the total number of employed Americans increases. Furthermore, the openings available depend more on turnover than anything else. Here we refer to people who retire or leave, thereby creating a job opening. Turnover in the U.S. *(for all jobs)* is more than 25% per year.

Another key thing to keep in mind is that people do have certain career situations that can and will get worse. In other words, the longer you wait to make a decision, the worse your situation is likely to become.

For example, the longer a person remains on the brink of losing a job, unhappy every day, under stress or unchallenged, the deeper the hole that person may dig for themselves. In short, the more aggravating their family and career situation may become.

If you wait and allow this to happen, the negative impact on your mental outlook can be severe. You will never be able to approach marketing yourself with the right frame of mind.

Then, there are some liabilities that only get worse with time. For example, if you have topped out, or if you have stayed in one industry or one company for a long time. Here you will get increasingly less marketable. Of course, age is a major liability that clearly gets more challenging with time. Things will only be more serious later on.

You also need to concern yourself with your personal achievements that may have been significant, but which can lose their impact. Take an example of a sales executive in a job for two years, who is not achieving very well. However, for the prior two years he had been a top achiever, received major awards and was on a high.

Obviously, for this man, as time goes on the impact of those earlier achievements will become less and less. And, unfortunately, if he stayed too long in his situation, he would become characterized by mediocrity rather than recognized by his most impressive achievements. With senior executives and high achievers, the impact factor is very important.

Sometimes people are on the horns of a dilemma ... in a quandary... perhaps uptight and in doubt. *Sometimes, it seems like we can't act on anything*. One thing for this person to keep in mind is the very fact that doing something will make you feel better about yourself, make you more productive and motivate you to achieve. We have found that taking action is often the only cure for anxiety.

Will the McKenzie Scott System Work for Everyone? The Answer Is No.

This system is for the vast majority of individuals anywhere who feel they have a record of achievement at professional, managerial or executive levels, and who believe they are qualified to seek a position from $60,000 to $500,000+ in the United States.

Furthermore, we believe there are no professional job seekers who could not increase their chances for reaching their goals by making aggressive use of the resources we provide. We have accepted as clients those who have significant challenges related to age, lack of formal education, longer term unemployment and other concerns.

However, some start out with such a high degree of difficulty and challenge, that even with the leverage provided by our resources, they stand a less than average chance for success in today's competitive environment. For example:

❑ People seeking relocation, but with no budget to travel to a new location for interviews

❑ People with very narrow geographical requirements in small second-tier markets

❑ People who are not legal to work in the U.S.

❑ Those with extreme specialization by function or industry where there is declining demand for their talents, and whose prospect for changing industries is less than average

❑ Those with a severe disability that prevents them from interviewing at employers' offices or speaking easily on the phone

❑ Those with poor educational credentials and limited achievements to compensate

❑ Those with significant age issues and no record of valuable contributions in demand today

❑ People who are not highly motivated or are reticent about embracing new directions

❑ And some who face substantial bias in the job market by virtue of personality, physical appearance, heavy accent, mental depression, medical or other factors beyond their control

People in these and similar categories need to consider that while our resources will enhance virtually anyone's chances, the odds of their being successful will still not be favorable in today's highly competitive climate.

Recapping Aspects of Our Service for You

Information gathering phase (online)

- Career history and marketability profile *(your career in review)*
- Personal issues profile *(for concerns we will address)*
- Marketability evaluation profile *(for marketability comparison)*
- Personal profile for new career environments
- Industry characteristics profile (*for surfacing new options)*

Knowing how to professionally job search

- Our handbook, Part II, on our job search system
- Our 3-day career advancement seminar online condensed into 4 hours of fast moving audio

Custom marketing plan that we create & present

- Our marketability comparison report
- Our personal career report
- Pinpointing your assets and transferable skills
- Solutions for handling any liabilities or concerns
- Your best industry options surfaced
- Short/long term goals established
- A step-by-step action plan for running your entire search. Presented privately and in writing

Professional resumes we create

- A universal resume for generating maximum activity
- A quick response resume for use without cover letters
- An electronic resume for using online
- Our sample package of outstanding letters is supplied

Basic resume distributions to get you started

- Up to 3,000 national recruiters—electronically
- Up to 200 local recruiters—by first class mail
- Up to 200 local venture capitalists—electronically
- Up to 200 local key employers—by first class mail
- Up to 200 local growth firms—by first class mail

Access to openings, leads and contacts

- You will have instant access to openings (including *Advertised Market Supersearch)* from 3,000 newspapers, from 100,000 employers, from 2,100 magazines, from 3,000 recruiters, from 250 leading job boards and full use of our interactive information services—with 24 to 48-hour service.
- Our guide to using our information center is supplied
- Our guide to databases and how to use them is supplied

Ongoing online support

- Our interactive information service online… with 24 to 48-hour response to requests virtually eliminates your need for doing any other research
- Our online job hunting support system with advanced interviewing and negotiation strategies

Ongoing team support

- An entire team of specialists is put at your disposal, dedicated to you and your job search. This team is available for any problem or concern, as well as ongoing coaching, mentoring and followup support.

Optional creative services

- Professional writing of an interview resume *(see pg. 72)*
- Professional writing of a CEO biography *(see pg. 72)*
- Professional drafting of 12 marketing letters *(see pg. 73)*

Optional added resume distribution services

- To 1,000 premier recruiters who do scanning
- Custom direct mail to employers or venture capitalists in packages of 1,000, 2,000 or 3,000 mailings

Optional board member mailings

- Custom written communications, under our letterhead, typically 12 contacts per week, for up to 16 weeks *(see pg. 107)*

If any client uses our system and fails to be closing in on attractive offers after 90-120 days, we offer a one-time guarantee.

In these situations, at their request, we will assign a new team, and have them develop an entirely new marketing plan, rewrite all resumes we prepared, and relaunch all electronic resume distributions. This has proven to be necessary in less than 2% of all engagements.

Success Is in Your Hands
Your Destiny Is Yours to Control

With our unique resources there might be a temptation to think they will carry the day, and that relatively little effort will be required on your part to uncover opportunities and win an attractive job.

For some people, the most highly marketable, our resources might in fact do just that. Contacts with recruiters and high probability employer targets could alone surface enough suitable opportunities, so their efforts may be relatively small.

We wish that all our clients could experience that. But through our regular staff followup and online tracking system, we closely monitor the activity of every client, and we have statistics that tell us otherwise.

We especially look at how often and how extensively they make use of our information center. The unfortunate truth is, *only 3% of our successful clients use the Center lightly*. Of our most successful clients, 92% used it extensively, 5% moderately.

The implications are clear. Similar to any other resources you might purchase to help you achieve a goal, no matter how effective they might have been for thousands of others, they will work for you only if you implement according to plan.

Attending the finest golf school will not lower your score unless you practice regularly. The most effective weight loss program works only if you faithfully adhere to what it requires in terms of exercise and food intake. The most rigorous physical conditioning program gets you in great shape only if you get to the gym and do the exercises on a regular basis.

Our resources have been compared by some to a Ferrari—a unique, finely tuned set of information and team resources that are powerful and can help get you where you want to go faster than any other resources known to job seekers. But you've got to get in and drive that Ferrari... and drive it well. And you've got to drive it fast to win the race.

Likewise, if you decide to make use of our extensive resources, it is your responsibility to make the most of them. You will need to access them on a daily basis, take advantage of the ability to quickly find information and contacts others cannot, and be as creative and aggressive as you need to be in order to surface the right opportunities.

The job market *is not* the same for everyone, and *no two people* have exactly the same marketability. The responses you get from your job market will tell you how active and aggressive you need to be.

Fortunately, our resources enable you to be active at any level of aggressiveness you require for success. But it is up to you to use them to that level—to drive our "Ferrari" as aggressively as you need in order to achieve your goals.

Introduction to Our Step-by-Step Guide to Using Our System—Expanded Edition

Once you've become a client and have completed your information profiles, you will receive the expanded edition of our system. Besides this material, it includes proprietary strategies you should know to help you make our system work to your maximum advantage. Here's a brief summary of the added information we cover.

The Seven Most Popular New Careers

Here we examine the seven most popular directions chosen by executives. These may supplement whatever ideas you already have developed.

Creating Your Own Job

Every year we are surprised by the increasing number of clients who report that their new jobs were created for them. Here, we review some of what we've learned.

Guidelines for Developing Your Best Stories

Here you find additional guidance and examples on developing the stories which are so critical to your communication strategy.

Maximizing Your Telephone Power

Here we deal with approaches for beginning your conversations... our keys for using the phone... tips for handling people who screen your call... and opening comments to make after you reach the right person.

McKenzie Scott Rules for Networking

Here we discuss our ways for addressing questionable references. We will share what we have learned about how to best handle them along with rules for getting the most out of networking.

Guidelines for Writing Superior Letters

Here you review what we have learned about how to make your letters into the most effective documents possible. Our philosophy on cover letters, letter-resumes, handwritten notes and more are covered.

McKenzie Scott Rules for Direct Mail

Here you learn our philosophy about selecting high probability targets and building your priority list. Our concept for classifying prospects is reviewed.

How to Read Your Interviewer

Wouldn't it be nice to be able to *"read"* everyone who interviews you... and to know, based upon their personality, the kind of candidate they prefer? Then, you could adapt your behavior to fit their preferences. As part of our service, we help each of our clients do just that. You will learn how to best understand your own style and how to use our profile system for reading everyone who interviews you.

How to Build Maximum Chemistry

With other talented competitors under consideration, you must have a strategy of coming out #1 among 10. To ensure this happens, your first step will be to build chemistry with everyone you meet. The system we have developed has worked for thousands of job seekers.

How to Overcome Objections

Your third key to interviewing is to be able to overcome objections in a seamless way. With today's competition, if you stumble, there are too many others the employer can turn to. So, why play this by ear?

When you are thrown objections, you will find that our process is easy-to-follow and will work almost every time. If you encounter a pattern of disappointment, our staff can be available to strategize or debrief every situation... and get things turned around. You'll also be provided with 100 top questions that have caught candidates off-guard, along with samples of suggested answers.

How to Project the Right Image

Overall impressions are established within the first few minutes of each of your interviews. Here, we suggest a number of guidelines to make sure you project your very best image.

Our Six-Step Negotiation Formula

Too many executives make the mistake of thinking they are experts in this unique arena. However, successful negotiators are the ones who are very prepared, and never argumentative or emotional. Thousands of people have achieved great success by sticking to our straightforward process. We also review all the different items that you might negotiate... review various negotiation situations... and provide phrases for you to use in your own negotiations. Classic letters that we have used for responding to offers and negotiating an increase are also supplied.

Building Your Will to Succeed

A positive attitude is the single most common thread among people who move quickly in the job market. It will enable you to separate yourself from thousands who simply give up or settle for less.

In this section we review ways for developing and maintaining positive beliefs about yourself... how you can quickly get rid of any negative concerns... how to set your expectations higher and put them to work... how you can project a positive attitude to everyone and how you can maximize your confidence and self-esteem.

Maximizing Our Information Center

Millions of dollars in investment and years of work have enabled us to pioneer what has been widely praised as the single most valuable job hunting tool ever created.

Besides acquainting you with our capabilities in depth, you will receive a color laminated guide for your ready reference to our information center throughout your search. You'll also receive our complete descriptive guide to all the databases we maintain for our clients' use.

Our Ongoing Relationship

This further briefs you on all the capabilities of the McKenzie Scott staff members who will be available to you throughout your search. We also review our ongoing client tracking and followup system, which has drawn the praise of many clients.

If you have received this book and are not a client of our firm, you can receive more information about our capabilities by calling Paul Mills, Sr. Vice President, at 800-320-1277.

McKenzie Scott, 7979 East Tufts Avenue Parkway, Ste. 1400, Denver, CO 80237 • 800-320-1277 • Fax 303-770-8639